Notes from the Ocean

A Celebration of Love

Joyful Awakening Books

Notes from the Ocean
A Celebration of Love

Dr. Paula Bromberg

Notes from the Ocean
A Celebration of Love
Copyright © 2023 by Dr. Paula Bromberg
First Edition
All Rights Reserved
Limited Edition

No part of this book may be used or reproduced in any manner whatsoever without written permission, except in the case of brief quotations embodied in critical articles and reviews.

For reproduction rights, contact
Dr. Paula Bromberg
E-mail: Goldoceandrive@gmail.com
Facebook:PaulaAmbikaBromberg

Publisher's Cataloging-in-Publication
Bromberg, Dr. Paula N.
Notes from the Ocean
A Celebration of Love
Dr. Paula N. Bromberg -- 1st Ed.
p. cm.
LCCN 2003112905
ISBN 978-0-9715474-0-7
1. Self-actualization. 2. Spiritual life.
3. Interpersonal relations. 4. New Age.
5. Personal growth. 6. Self-help.
I. Title.
BF637.S4B76 2004   158.1
                           QBI03-700680

also available as an E-book

Printed in the United States of America

Photos: Dr. Paula Bromberg and Friends
Book design: South Beach Grafix/Dr. Paula Bromberg
Cover photograph: Dr. Paula Bromberg

Also by Dr. Paula Bromberg:

The Way of the Lover – A Way of Understanding
The Fifth Way – Life at its Best, 2020
    HardCover—Limited Edition

Tantra, East West, Past/Present: Living Presence, 1995
Endeavor, A Journal in the Sufi tradition, 1993

Sacred Psychology: The Path of the Heart, 1989

Notes from the Ocean
A Celebration of Love

The Message: Awakening into Love, a life saturated with song and understanding is beautiful: listen to the song that resonates within you and discover where the sacred and the everyday intersect.

A resonance of ocean resides in each of us—may *Notes from the Ocean* carry the salt breeze and music across the land, the harmonious symphony of the universe, life itself as music, each of us embodied as our particular distinct musical note.

The Subject Tonight Is Love

The subject tonight is Love
And for tomorrow night as well.
As a matter of fact,
I know of no better topic
For us to discuss

Until we all die!

—Hafiz

If the Beloved said,
pay homage to everything
that has helped you
enter my arms.

There would not be one experience of my life,
not one thought, not one feeling,
not any act,
I would not bow to.

—Rumi

Contents

Notes from the Ocean vi

The Subject Tonight Is Love vii

Acknowledgements... x

Praise for Notes from the Ocean.................. xii

Testimonial: The Work Works xviii

About the Cover... 1

Introduction: The Invitation..........................4

Part One

The World: Life Through the Lens of Love ... 16

Song of the Sea... 18

Emunah: The Invisible 28

Lamentation from Sorrow to Celebration..... 34

Songs We are Music!.................................... 42

Part Two

Ocean of Consciousness 56

Questions... 61

Contents

Deep Listening 76
Understanding 81
Suffering 89
Practice 106
Ocean 120
The Children 128
The Brain, The Mind, Consciousness 137
Attention 149
Spiritual Friendship 158
Maturity 165
Death and Compassion 170

Books and Authors I Treasure 178
Singing Creation Into Being 180
Thank You 182
Further Continuing Work 185
About the Author 186

Acknowledgements

A Dedication of Gratitude and Praise

To the beautiful beings who touch my heart, a practice of love.

Grateful for the deepening conversations that feed my soul.

To the Ocean, my sanctuary, and the music that is the courier of joy and sorrow.

To Sashie, my beloved soul-mate: our blessing to recognize each others true face: the music for my heart is the sound of your breath.

To Paula who has embarked on this continuous journey of risk and consequence, a privilege of aliveness.

Acknowledgements

To the beautiful beings who open their heart in conversation on our enlivened journey of love.

A deep bow to the physical discomforts and pain that has been life's companion as well as to the joy, song and experiences that penetrate into the core of existence.

Living into the given sangha names: *Joyful Awakening, Ambika Ma, Paula Nada*: who is the I that carries these names?

To meet life with an open heart awakening into wisdom, wholeness and integrity towards myself and others.

And always to the spirit and force that has persisted and continued and continues, this presence that reflects all that is.

Praise for Notes from the Ocean

Your glorious tome arrived and sits by my bed and I am wading through the introductory pages so much is in these books that I will be wading for a long time. They are very beautiful books with sublime Buddha, the Ocean, and the sublime soul behind it. I feel honored to receive, read and be invited to write comments. Your books and writing are extraordinary, beautiful crafted and I am glad to have *The Way of the Lover* and *Notes From The Ocean*. Both are written with such divine perfection. May love and divinity suffuse everything you do. I recommend both of your books to anyone who wishes to live within and be uplifted by the beautiful poetic artistry and heartfelt wisdom of your writing and teaching.

—Dr. Janine Canan M.D.
poet, Psychiatrist, essayist, story-writer, translator, and editor. Wrote and published 25 books including 5 books/compilations of the teachings of Guru Mata Amritananda Mayi

Your book—what a delight! What joy! And wisdom!
—Carol Donahoe
visual artist living at Paramanhansa Yogananda Self-Realization Center Fellowship

Paula's inner processing comes from her own self-exploration and not the reiteration of others thoughts/experiences, but with a need to understand for herself. She has used her devastation to fire her own work. Your book is on our table and has become a daily source of a heart reminder. You have created comprehensive and personal revelations of how you got to where you are. You have thrived, are alive with a soft understanding. You continue to give with your bounty, all you can of your beneficial being. Your light is shining through

Praise

for any who have tired of darkness, With the highest regard, respect and heartfelt love, I bow.

— Elaine Marchese, Connecticut Book Store Owner

I treasure your masterpiece The Way of the Lover and love to read parts of it as soul food when I'm tired of answering thousands of letters. Thank you, thank you, thank you!!! Blessings on the first College/University based program in this country training hospice workers that we co-created to assist beautiful souls to embrace their transition. Thank you for teaching and writing!

—Elisabeth Kübler-Ross, M.D.
author, psychiatrist, creator of the hospice movement, revolutionized the care of the terminally ill, a pioneer in near-death studies, inducted into the National Women's Hall of Fame

Paula Bromberg is a genuine big-hearted woman who has a rare and profound intelligence and a deep understanding of authentic compassion.

—Natalie Goldberg
renowned writing teacher, best-selling author of 16 books, painter, retreat leader, filmmaker, zen practitioner

The reminder of Paula's commitment to live her creative potential is what you receive in this book, the culmination of her life work. Paula is connected to the Source, empowering her to live her creative potential. May her journey lead her-lead her-lead her. Her book, The Way of the Lover, is a true teaching.

—Edith Wallace, M.D., Ph.D.
author, Jungian analyst who received her analytic training directly from Carl Jung M.D., prize winning painter, world-wide teacher

Dr. Paula is a passionate soul whose vision penetrates the core mystery of what it means to be human.

—Rabbi Michael Ziegler
founder and leader of Song of Songs Minyan, guest faculty Naropa University, book reviewer

♪ *Notes from the Ocean*

In my experience, Paula Bromberg is an extraordinarily knowledgeable Teacher who speaks with the authority of the heart and is gifted with the ability to articulate and clarify her deep understanding of the logos thus making it available to seekers and inquirers.

—José Stevens. Ph.D.
international lecturer, psychologist, corporate team builder, Shaman, author of 20 books

I have known Dr. Paula Bromberg for over 40 years. Thus I have been witness to a magnificent tapestry. Fierce warrior, yet gentle spirit. Seeker, teacher and disciple. The wide eyes and open heart of a child. She teaches us that everything is sacred yet nothing exists. Paula is both illumination and reflection. This book, The Way of the Lover, is a miracle.

—Rona Lieberman, M.D.
Physician practicing responsible medicine for over 35 years.

To aspire towards higher consciousness and spiritual growth defining and understanding one's authentic self is a major component of paramount importance. Dr. Bromberg's book The Way of the Lover is an insightful and informative tool and as a co-companion can guide and support the enfoldment of this learning process, which is ongoing, joyous and eternal. Namaste.

—Mara Howard
yoga and meditation teacher

Paula Bromberg is giftedly willing and able to look at love and all of its expressions with more clarity and honesty than most people would ever dare.

—David Deida
acclaimed author of 10 books, a founder of Integral Institute, teacher and researcher at University of California Medical School and École Polytechnique, Paris, France

Praise

I have learned much from Paula Bromberg's grasp of human types, as well as her moral sincerity.

—Kabir Helminski, Ph.D
Sufi teacher, psychologist, author and translator of Sufi literature, Shaikh of the Mevlevi order of Sufi which traces to Rumi, tours with the whirling dervishes of Turkey, director of the Threshold Society

Some people write a book in a month and some in a year and others take their time, so the book grows as they do, until we have a living document of a life well-lived and well-considered. Such is this book by Dr. Paula Bromberg, The Way of the Lover, rich in her knowledge, abundant with her wisdom, and redolent with her deep understanding. Socrates said, "The unexamined life is not worth living." Paula's life has been overflowing with self-examination, and through the salient processes she offers, now a significant resource for those who wish to know themselves. Her brilliant opus is a work of art and courage.

Reading Notes from the Ocean, the play of words within words, sounds as music and poetry; teachings about the origin of sound vibrations creating the universe and becoming words. I am enjoying the way music, the ocean, sound soul, the meaning of your name and all the poetry are woven together in Notes from the Ocean. I think of all the studying you have done and feel admiration for what you know and how you put ideas together. You are an amazing woman Paula and have had an extraordinary life. I love the tidbits about your family that come through this book and I must say you have a unique style that's all your own. Thank You.

—Aile Shebar
creative writing teacher, writing coach, editor and author

Notes from the Ocean, A Celebration of Love is an Inspirational Meditation on Love, Life and Song. Dive in. Sing Along!
—Cantor Robert Weiner, Ph.D. Jones Professor of History, Jewish Chaplain Emeritas

Paula Bromberg's The Way of the Lover *in clear, simple terms brings tools for self-actualization and empowerment. Bromberg's book is poised to replace conventional psychotherapy and religion as the true journey, the way of choice.*

—Larry Chang
author, director of Gnosophia Publishers

Paula Bromberg is a true intellect and a profound healer. Her teaching is magical and has helped me in my work with addicts using a spiritual approach. Deeply rooted in a massive knowledge of people and in life, her book The Way of the Lover *is bold and beautiful.*

—Kerry Riordan
addiction specialist counselor, New York, Puerto Rico

I have known Paula Bromberg since elementary school days. Both of us traveled healing and spiritual paths. I established a Tibetan Medical Center and Paula became the on-call therapist for my clients in the New York and Massachusetts Centers. A brilliant team—Dr. Paula, Dr. Yeshi Dhonden and Dr. Marsha. Reading her book, The Way of the Lover *is like sitting with a master: inspiring, uplifting, educational and enlightening. You must own this book, and carry it around, to actually use.* The Way of the Lover *fills an important need, finally a guide to understand who we are and how to love.*

—Dr. Marsha Woolf
founder and director of New World Medical Center and Alternative Resources, director of Menla Tibetan Medical Institute, author, naturopath, worked for over 25 years with Dr. Yeshi Dhonden, personal senior physician to His Holiness the 14th Dalai Lama

When I write these words about Dr. Paula I want to say thank you. They come straight from my heart with endless gratitude.

Praise

Paula Bromberg's book The Way of the Lover *is transformational in its nature to understand more of what one refers to as "Self." It is a reference I continue to explore, encouraging me to become more curious and introspective in my daily life's work and as a yoga practitioner and teacher.*

Life unfolds in mysterious, beautiful ways to show us why and how we are living in this lifetime. Paula's guidance to support, transform, encourage, and lift, is a gift I will always hold in the depths of my heart. I have gone to places in my own soul I never imagined, and my love, joy, and gratitude for my life has never felt stronger and content. Paula's personal gift to this lifetime in giving unconditional love, and seeing each individual truly for who they are, has been instrumental to my life's work. Having Paula as a mentor is indescribably precious.

—Meaghan Tozzi
yoga teacher, artist, designer, mother

A lifes work
A true understanding of the path
The recognition of the illusion
of our separateness
This is her guide book
and the tools that are needed
to plow the mind
into a vibrational frequency
of the real
Love upon love

—Charles Soloway, Udbodha
musical artist, created *Awakening*

♪ *Notes from the Ocean*

Testimonial
The Work Works

Paula challenged me and gave me the courage to step into myself. Throughout the process I learned to truly be in the moment. The joy and freedom I feel is a gift I am grateful for everyday. She saved my life. She gave me my life.

I have worked with Paula for twelve years. Over those years, she challenged me and gave me the courage to be me. In the process I learned to love my nature and respect myself. With her guidance, I had the health, clarity, and energy to raise a beautiful family.

When I hear Paula's voice on the phone I know I am going to be ok. The work isn't always easy, but under her guidance, I have learned to love my nature. I crave her wisdom, clarity, and problem solving. She's both held my hand and kicked me in the butt. Because of Paula, I have been able to raise two beautiful children and keep a marriage strong. I'm also just more joyful, a gift I am grateful for everyday.

—Elizabeth Clair Flood
author, editor, photographer

Just sitting here at sunset, loving you. Hope you feel it. You've given me the greatest gift of my life, which is my life right now in this moment. I hold you in the same regard I hold my birth mother, in total gratitude for giving me an opportunity of a beautiful life. The beauty of my love and life is because of you.

I can never express my deep gratitude because not a day goes by that you don't wander (or firmly roll) into my thoughts. Thank you dear

Testimonial

Paula for everything. My life is because of you. I love you now and always, and my children also know your presence because of the way I parent them. A deep exhale and deep bow to you, Paula my beloved mamaji.

—Amanda Botur
yoga teacher, leads yoga teacher trainings, masters in traditional chinese medicine, classical homeopath, songwriter, musician—album *Confluence*

Paula is my sage, a voice to my soul and heart. She has brought a voice to a perspective on myself that I wouldn't have otherwise. I am eternally grateful for her in my life.

Amanda, my wife, introduced me to Dr. Paula as we started working through our stories and problems as a married couple. She has been there through thick and thin, with guidance, compassion, and humor to our individual stories. She has come to our collective defenses and our indifference throughout our 18 years of marriage. Paula has added a strength and significance to bond our family journey.

—Freddie Botur
conservation pioneer and adviser, cowboy, cattle rancher, Cottonwood Ranch, climber and Alpinist, asset manager, entrepreneur

I have worked with other therapists in the past, but none of them enabled me to transcend my history and the pain entangled there in the way that Paula has.

Paula is exceedingly wise and compassionate. Her comprehension of an individual's particular nature, what I understand to be the truth of who a person is beyond her conditioning, is profound. With Paula's gentle yet powerful support I have come to recognize and embrace my true nature and this has given me much relief from suffering as well as enormous peace.

♪ *Notes from the Ocean*

I consider Paula to be a teacher and mentor guiding me on an intimate journey of self-discovery. I am deeply grateful for her in my life.

—Cynthia S. DaCosta
psychotherapist, horse trainer, philanthropic foundation / grant-maker

Paula Bromberg has given me one of the greatest gifts of my life— she gave me back myself. I began working with her over 20 years ago when I was emotionally lost, in unloving relationships, unhappy. Paula, through deep compassion, humor, and pushing me to do my work, helped me peel back the layers and patterns I'd hidden behind for decades. I began to re-discover my true self and, with that, true peace. I am now a joyful person, almost all the time, and even when facing several tragedies at once a few years ago, I knew I would be ok. And I was ok. Because Paula had given me the gift of myself. And isn't that really what we are all searching for? Isn't that where all our life's purposes and work and joy reside?

Paula is both a demanding teacher, always insisting I own every situation, every choice in my life. And never allowing me to blame another. She is also a deeply loving and hilariously funny teacher too. 21 years after meeting her, I still call her whenever there's turmoil in my life and her easy laugh and deep insight make me instantly feel better. Paula's work is so unusual in its depth, but also in its sensitivity. My emotional health doesn't look like my friend's health or my child's health. Paula leads us each to our own mountain top, and each peak is beautiful and each peak is different. She works with me, as me. And maybe most importantly of all, she never loses the connection between health and spirituality. She is grounded and present, but she always gently reminds me that I am part of something much larger than myself. That spiritual connection, coupled with a deep sense of knowing and loving who

Testimonial

I am, has created a joy in my life, the depth of which still surprises me. It is resilient, it is generous and it is loving, because when we are connected to our true, healed selves and to the limitless love of the universe, life is beautiful.

Paula has made me rich because I have peace, I have compassion. And I have joy. I will always have profound gratitude and love for her and how she has enriched my life.

—Heather Pentland, L.Ac.
created New Leaf Healing Center, trained in China and New Mexico in traditional chinese medicine, acupuncture and herbal medicine

Every week I am grateful for my time with Paula. She has helped me through some of life's most difficult bumps and helped me to feel more calm, grateful and happy. She has helped me parent with more grace and love and to see some of the most beautiful and hidden parts of my children.

Dr. Paula pushes me when I am ready for growth and is gentle and reassuring when I am not. Her influence on my life and my family's life has been an incredible gift.

—Kristen Revill
B.A. Dartmouth College M.A. Stanford University, currently teaching on the science faculty at Jackson Hole Community School

Little did I know that when I contacted Dr. Paula Bromberg over 13 years ago how much of an impact on my life that initial call would have. I had sought counseling a few other times in my life so I was not a total stranger to entering therapy. In an hour over the phone, I could see my relationship issues and struggles more clearly. Working with her was different. She was not going to tell me what I thought I wanted or needed to hear. What ensued was a working journey into a better understanding of who I was and seeing why and how I reacted to situations that were presented in my life.

We used the Enneagram and other tools to help me explore and accept my true nature. I slowly began embracing that true nature. Stopped pushing against it and criticizing it. I shifted how I began to see and accept others, celebrating their differences, but keeping myself on course, my true way of being.

On I traveled staying in the relationship, keeping my professional practice going, navigating my father's death, my mother's illness, and her passing. That brought sibling challenges and how to negotiate what I needed. Each life event brought a chance to work on myself. I moved to another state, creating another phase of life. My beloved dog passed. There were professional challenges and opportunities to shift my business. As I grew and matured my marriage relationship changed and ended. As I enter this new phase of my life, I am forever in deep gratitude to Dr. Paula.

—Marybeth Minter, DVM
classical veterinary homeopath and nutritional counselor, teacher and lecturer, Mariposa veterinary services

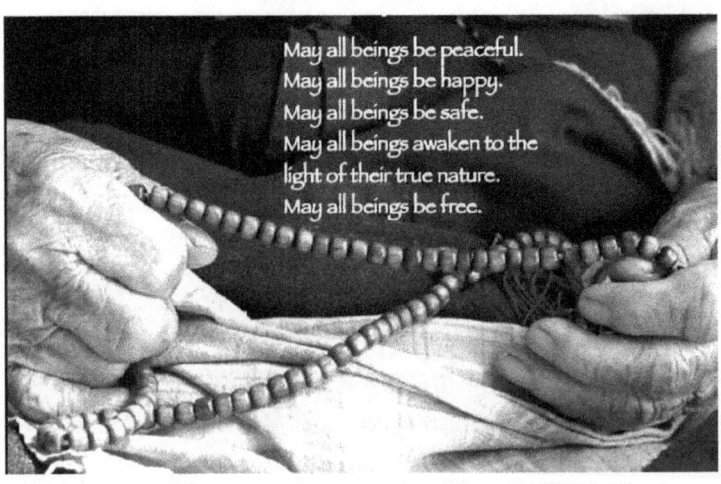

About the Cover

I took the photo from the 32nd floor of a local hotel in Fort Lauderdale with my IPhone. Choosing this ocean photo among many of the daily pictures I take because of the depth and angles and perspective, appreciating that I could see perspective since it's something that was lost to me as a child created through an accident which eventually took away my ability to see dimensionally. Life ultimately became a Grandma Moses painting gifting me with my own unique vision of seeing. Always a prize in our limitations that open and express our personal path of wonder. A child's way of looking at life.

The letters surfacing from the ocean spell Love/Beloved, Hebrew letters that I designed for my wedding ring many years ago. *Aleph Bet Vav Hay.* Tradition and imagery say that holy letters have been fashioned out of black fire upon white fire. The infinite and finite, vessels to carry us across the ocean. Both water and fire sustain and destroy life. Letters and ocean, the blueprint of creation: a divine presence, and to liberate the sparks through our recognition of what is sacred; our task here to repair the brokenness through the musicality the melody—sound vibration and harmony. Birds and animals repeat this. We feel it in the atmosphere, engraved and etched, are we open to hear the orchestration? The breath remains as life. Blessings sing: celebration nourished from the water, sun—notes from the ocean rising. The Hebrew Aleph-Bet, a name derived from the first two letters, one of the oldest in the world are considered to be a blue-print, building blocks creating the world, each of the 22 letters a key.

Hidden within each letter lies the mystery, its vitality,

carriers of genetic coding, the creation of language, liturgy, notes: a dynamic force that reflects life itself, the precious jewels a bouquet. Is the ocean a blueprint for humanity with holy letters musically rising? A window to the soul that shines in all corners of our life. Each detail of creation has the potential of infinite meaning, beneath the surface—deeply placed in the ocean waiting to be revealed are the endless meanings. We are offered the tools, we work with them, in doing this we open gates to enter sacred inner spaces raising the secular to the sacred.

The Letters ו ה ב א

Aleph Bet Hay Vav spell *Ahavah*: Love *Ahuvah*: Beloved.

Aleph is the first letter, the soundless image of beginnings. Space-less and present, affirming something from nothing. It has no sound. And what is sound? Is it outside or inside? To understand the mystery of sound is to know the mystery of the whole universe.

Bet is the second letter of the Aleph-Bet and represents the beginning of duality, from unity and now there are two. Yin and yang, light and dark, yes and no—we have the possibility to move further to experience the oneness beyond all duality. Bet is the structure, the house, the body which contains the spirit. A house anchored upon this earth. A home with blessings to remember the unity and oneness of the silent Aleph. The ocean of love that enters our heart.

The fifth letter *Hay*—the sound of breathing out, often said to mean *behold, breath, look*. Depicted as a person with arms raised as beholding something or someone: Hay stands for divine manifestation. Breath is life. Conscious breathing, transporting energy from one world to another, being

About the Cover

awake to the breath brings us into the present moment; the experience of being one with all things and beings. Breathing, a continuous flow from birth to death, connecting us to our body, to the universe, is the bridge.

Vav the sixth letter is the connector and binds everything together in our universe. We are beads strung on a single thread and Vav is the hook that joins, that binds. Love towards each other is the crowning jewel. To understand something we first see its connection to a larger whole. And when doors open we expand and sanctify life to become one with humanity, interdependent. And we see that our happiness is not separate from the happiness of others. This quality of connectedness, which first originates from an authentic self-connection, expands outwards, honors our differences and has a reverence for all of life. *Vav*

Life is lyrical. Letters rising from the ocean, we sing. Listen, hear—a letter speaks, emanating vibratory power: audible, visible, perceptible. The first sign of life is the audible expression, or sound that is the letters, the word. The sacred name, the word—the soul and vibration contained in the letters.

Notes from the Ocean—letters of fire, dance. The ocean of love—even one note dipped and rising from the ocean of love that penetrates enables us to enter the temple of our own heart for us to hear the music. The music are notes strung on a single thread of love.

Nachman knew what power the letters possessed. Each letter holy, having a personality, a life of it's own.
—C. Leviant

Introduction

The Invitation

Wherever you are and whatever you do, be in love. It is love that holds everything together, and it is the everything also. Love rests on no foundation. It is an endless Ocean, with no beginning or end. —Rumi

Writing and publishing *The Way of the Lover,* a 1529 page manuscript, I certainly had not considered writing another book. I had imagined that book to be the full completion and expression. *Aha,* said existence, *you have more to live*; impermanence is a powerful teacher. What now appears in this life as it is in the present moment: ocean, beach walks, smiles, joy, sunrise, a body that expresses impermanence, touching hearts, sorrow, music, writing, deep conversation: life is a practice towards waking up. How to create a world where reverence, kindness and compassion in relation to ourselves, each other and this magnificent earth and ocean share our common humanity? And, we are told in every generation there is unfinished work for us to complete, as well as to leave work for the next generation. *L'dor v'dor* from generation to generation, our communal love to strengthen the bonds between and among all generations, blessings to receive this legacy and to become a custodian of holy wisdom.

The wings we have are so fragile they can break from just one word, or a glance void of love. —St. Catherine of Sienna

Introduction

And so here I am continuing, receiving the generosity of my foremothers and forefathers this task of privilege: writing/speaking from the heart. No longer an earnest, eager, enthusiastic, risk-taking youngster, now sobered from the sorrows; impermanence rings loudly as I escort, accompany, walk my beloveds and myself home. Change and becoming. Sorrow and joy, celebration and surrender; *Yes, this is a beautiful world to be born into if you don't mind happiness not always being so very much fun.* Maturity—and with that comes the responsibility to bear witness to the grief, joys, the stories, the narratives of lives that touch this life, as well as beyond.

Reb Zalman said *Into your blessed hands*: yes, within my hands, within my arm spam, living into the stream of service leads me to the ocean of truth. I invite you to bring your spirit of wonder as you enter into this journey named *Notes from the Ocean, a Celebration of Love.*

What is there but this present moment, redolent with rich treasures—aliveness, suffering, love, yearning, beauty, music, because, wrote poet Ferlinghetti: *the world is a beautiful place to be born into if you don't mind happiness not always being so very much fun. If you don't mind a touch of hell now and then just when everything is fine because even in heaven they don't sing all the time.*

My cell phone rings with Louis Armstrong reminding me: *I see trees of green, red roses too I see them bloom for me and you And I think to myself What a wonderful world. I see skies of blue and clouds of white The bright blessed days, the dark sacred nights And I think to myself What a wonderful world. The colors of the rainbow So pretty in the sky Are also on the faces of people going by I see friends shaking hands saying, 'How do you do?' They're really saying, 'I love you'.*

This very body the earth, this very body the Buddha, so simple; our experience of being alive is the blessing, the privilege, the prize.

I cherish the writing experience; concise, precise, words to mean what I say, hearing an intimate voice, musical; we have been trained to read for comprehension. Let us also read for rhythm, poetry, tone and sound, the heartbeat that gives meaning to our world. Writing is music, is celebration, is the harmony of the breath of the writer/musician. Life works as the rhythmic movement of all that is; light, pulse, frequency, vibration. Throughout the ages the great prophets, mystics and illuminated souls have been musicians. They expanded into a universe of harmonious sound. Let us become musical in our life, with our thoughts, words, phrasing and actions. This creates a harmonious world of appreciation and beauty—all that is here in this world of vibration light and frequency: to become in tune with universal harmonic spheres.

Many say that life entered the human body by the help of music, but the truth is that life itself is music. —Hafiz

Introduction

We live in a world full with cliches, misunderstandings, slogans; peopled with empty words and crystalized others. How to uplift without crawling into untamed, untrained minds, not to be stirred by the waves, not to get caught in the current and carried away, rather to stay with the ocean; this is the real practice, and all life is a practice. Let's practice love, playfulness, let's practice waking up, kindness, joyful compassion, meaning what we say as we move forward into true maturity.

Every circumstance that arises offers a possibility of choice, risk, decision, as well as consequence. Is this moment received with a question, embraced, regardless to my opinion as to whether I imagined I wanted or know how to use it?

We are the net. Soul is the ocean we are in, but we cannot hold onto it. We cannot own any part of what we swim within, the mystery we love so. Yet the longing we feel is because of soul. To some degree we are what we are longing for. Some part of the ocean swims inside the fish. In Plotinus's view the visible universe—the entire cosmos, nature, ourselves, and all that we do—is a net thrown into the ocean of soul. 'because it has no size, the Soul's nature is sufficiently ample to contain the whole cosmic body in one and the same grasp.' —Coleman Barks

We all have our stories, our narratives, mementos of joy as well as sorrow. Death and birth, celebration, dance and song. Loss and reminder, high points, in-breath and exhalation. And now this exhalation: the birthing of a book: the arias, the chants, the notes: musical as well as pages of written words that originate from early wounding through to today's well-being.

My father, Manuel, was an avid note keeper. He wrote daily reminders and notes to himself as well as to me and to my sister Iris. *Remember!* or *Think!* he would preface each page and then proceed. To pick up the laundry, to smile, to help your mother; notes from the front line. Little did I know that years later I would enlarge upon this early teaching and make notes to myself, to the day, remembrances and musings, from the banal insignificance of a thought to mull over chew on and hopefully digest for the mundane is the profound—to conversing with the universe, the language of nature—opening to the force beyond myself, the inner part of self that is sound and light. And I continue this learned practice. Thoughts and notes jotted down, tucked away, sometimes trotted out and oftentimes thrown away. Everything expresses its meaning.

Music filled my home. Adele Rosalinde my mother, named after a character in *Die Fleidermaus*, a high-spirited operetta composed by Johann Strauss, with waltz and polka variation set in Vienna. Both of my grandmothers of Jewish heritage arriving from Europe by boat with scant knowledge of English hummed as they walked through their days. Humming tunes and

Introduction

melodies mostly unrecognizable, low singing sounds peacefully filling the air. I found their melodic tunes comforting.

The name chosen for me in this lifetime Paula/ Yiddish-Hebrew name *Pesha* from *Pey* or *Peh* meaning *mouth*, to speak; the mouth brings reality into being. How we speak creates invisible vibrations, produces an atmosphere through sound vibrations that is harmonious or disagreeable. Words are utilitarian, we learn to move beyond the letters. Before the word exists sound is needed. We alter the atmosphere through our emanations which affects whatever is around us; when we emanate joy we infect others, a chain reaction of joy ensues. Every word carries a value, a tone and creates an effect on life. Words matter! What we say can bring people together, shower blessings, but also might nurture deception, be destructive, dangerous. Spoken words are considered in certain mythologies to have the power to create worlds, creatures and human beings. They are containers and contents with energy that can heal, harm, humiliate, move hearts; their echos continue and continue.

Speech has power. Words do not fade. What starts out as a sound, ends in a deed. —Abraham Joshua Heschel

For us to transform a sound into a word we use the mind to give meaning to the sound. There is rhythm and musicality, a quality when we speak that carries aliveness or deadness. Before the word reaches us there is an invisible link, a dance that has the possibility to connect, to move us towards a new direction. To speak, to honor, encourage what is sacred is our elevated task. This is mantra, koan, repetitive chant, kirtan, all creating vibrations in the essence of our being. How to communicate in this way is miraculous.

To me, the greatest pleasure of speaking and writing is not what it's about, but the music the words make.
—Truman Capote

Pey is the seventeenth letter of the Hebrew alphabet. The design of the pey is a mouth and the gematria—assigning and adding up the numerical value to a word with its hidden meaning—of pey is eighty. *When one is eighty years old, we reach a special strength,* as it is said in *Ethics of the Fathers*. That ability to communicate is the essential aspect of eighty's particular proficiency. The mysticism of number is about rhythm and harmony. How we use our mouth, our speech—do we praise and lift others or do we denigrate and gossip? Every day is our opportunity to stretch and lift, to make the world whole. In this way we fulfill the purpose through transforming nature to make the world a better place to live. How can the power of our speech be a source of strength for others?

My middle name, Nada means *nothing* and is the Sanskrit word for *sound* or *tone* the hidden energy that connects the outer and inner cosmos, the entire universe consisting of sound vibrations called *nada*.

This is considered the sound from which the universe emanated and represents the fundamental oneness of all creation. Every moment that springs forth from life is vibration, within one vibration are created many vibrations, as motion causes motion, life eventually loses its initial silence. On the plane of Nada which is sound, vibration causes diversity of tone. In other words consciousness bears witness to its own voice. That is why it is said that music is the expression of the soul or spirit.

Music fills the infinite between two souls.
—Rabindranath Tagore

Necha, the Yiddish of my middle name Nada is from Neshamah and means breath, is the life-force or animating spirit, the divine soul referring to the essence of a person, our truest self. The sound, the rhythm, the vowels as well as the root from which our name is derived is a bridge connecting life to consciousness.

Our name is a message, its meaning once we investigate it opens worlds of deeper understanding to who we are and our purpose. Our name is important to our destiny and well-being and paves the way for the life steps, the direction we take and our future, a connection to our identity and individuality, carrying deep personal cultural familial and historical connections. Historically names have served as a fingerprint to one's identity. Not only do the syllables of our name hold a resonance sound that is powerful to the ear but also our name has a meaning that defines us. There is a treasure in our name and that preciousness lies in its meaning.

Words are things. Some day we'll be able to measure the power of words. They are things that get on the walls. They get in your wallpaper. They get in your rugs, in your upholstery, and your clothes, and finally in you.
—Maya Angelou

To know this world as sound we hear the blades of grass singing—the ancients have always known that the world is sound, rhythm and vibration. Cultures throughout the world describe how we choose pre-birth agreements when entering the world. We prepare the spiritual blueprint before we descend into matter as a script to enter this stage of life. Unraveling to understand the meaning and purpose as designed through our name adds a dimensional level to the significance of our purpose here on earth. Plotinus, third century Greece, wrote that *each soul selects its body, birthplace, and circumstances of life. Then as if a herald were summoning it the soul comes down and goes into the appropriate body.*

I remember taking a deep breath the day I asked Sri Mata Amritanandamayi Ma, the Mother, Amma, for a name. My mind traveled the distance of possibilities. Would she call me *Running Deer* or *Babbling Brook?* I hoped not. We gazed deeply as I melted into her embrace, my thoughts and concerns and mental chatter vanishing in her smile. *Ambika—Ambika*

Introduction

Ma she whispered into my ear, written in Sanskrit by Swami Amritaswarupananda, sitting by her side. Ambika—mother goddess, mother of the universe. I cherished the given name, Amma's vision, and held it in my heart until I met the precious innocent fragile Vizsla puppy—gifted to me from the stars. I knew that once named I would continue to see myself each moment that I called her *Ambika*, and also felt that I would be kind and tender to her preciousness as a tribute to Amma and to my own holiness. And I was. Each time I said *Ambika* I was calling myself—seeing myself in her gentle ways—a reminder and reflection. A true practice, to own myself as that. A reflection of pure divinity.

Our name transmits its meaning, points a direction towards the context and significance of our life purpose. The symbols are clear once we open and dive deeper. Our name is a veil, a challenge to look behind what appears as substantial and unchanging. Who is this I called Paula Nada? We have a name, a family name, a country name. And still, this existence is made up of sound, of subtle electrical vibrations. We say and lift up, to raise them, the names of those departed—offering dignity and remembrance. To be named is to be identified, to be seen, creating an energy force. Once the inner melody of our being is heard life becomes harmonious.

The name is of tremendous significance: it is closing accounts with the old, getting out of the old continuity.

♪ *Notes from the Ocean*

The name is the only continuity: everything else goes on changing, only the name remains continuous, and because of the name, the fallacy exists that we are not changing. The child changes into a young man or young woman, the young person changes into an old person, life changes into death. Everything goes on changing, it is a flux. Only this name remains static creating a great illusion: that gives you the idea as if you are permanent.
—Bhagwan Shree Rajneesh, Osho

It's the notes in the heart that have inspired me to proceed, and the beautiful beings who have touched my soul, enhanced my life and are a symphony orchestrating a wheel spin throughout this lifetime. Some have names, some remain nameless, from Rumi and Hafiz to the passerby on the beach, a traveler in the ocean as I make my beloved ocean walk, as well as the voices through the phone line that share their lives longings and stories over the years, unraveling to find their own heartsong.

Music is the basis of the whole creation. In reality the whole of creation is music, and what we call music is simply a miniature of the original music, which is creation itself expressed in tone and rhythm. —Hazrat Inayat Khan

Our ancestors believed that music had the power to harmonize the soul in a way that traditional medicine could not! —Gao Yuan

Part One

The World

Life Through the Lens of Love

Part One

You look around and you see a world that cannot be made sense of. You either raise your fists or you sing, Hallelujah. I try to do both. —Leonard Cohen

Distilled, the essence of a lifetime of teachings, a living testament to navigate this voyage. Each of us has our own unique limp, scars, stories that we tell or not. All birthright is a beginning. To make the world holy—liberation is a human story and at the heart of every story we extract wisdom and lean into love. Wanting to keep our mind in motion, to meet us where we are, like a pearl rolling in a golden bowl; if we want a pearl we dive deeply. Yes, there is nourishment in the broken places—now to be strong at the cracked places, to sing *Hallelujah* and redeem the brokenness of the world, we make peace with our fractured parts, concealed beauty, and have the courage to gain a sense of the mystery that animates all lifetimes. May these words empower, open doors and windows. To make the invisible visible, there is a bridge from my heart to your heart.

The Game: *To penetrate into the essence of all being and significance and to release the fragrance of that inner attainment for the guidance and benefit of others—by expressing in the world of forms, truth, love, purity, and beauty—this is the sole game which has intrinsic and absolute worth. All other happenings, incidents and attainments in themselves can have no lasting importance.* —Meher Baba

♪ *Notes from the Ocean*

Song of the Sea

The strongest and sweetest songs yet remain to be sung.
—Walt Whitman

Maori Aboriginals, indigenous people, stored knowledge and information in songlines. They encoded their stories, thoughts and understanding into song and dance. Not writing down prolonged, strengthened their memory bank. Relying on record, note-keeping can diminish our ability to remember and to be present to the vitality of each moment. Ancient indigenous cultures have used sophisticated oral memory systems, and people remembered countless details, which was the purpose of the songlines. Repeated regularly in ceremony and tradition this way of being has maintained cultures throughout millennium.

The pueblo culture passing their stories on through generations have maintained a minimum of seven varieties of corn for hundreds of years through anecdotes of corn maidens, beautiful women images each wearing a different color, personifying the bounty of life-giving corn that grows in six colors. Their presence symbolized the prayer for corn and a bountiful harvest, the divine gift of the growing and harvesting of corn, sustenance, staff of life, a gift from the Great Spirit to Native American peoples. Corn maidens honor Mother Earth and her continuing ability to feed her children; as the corn maidens sang their songs of faith and love it is said that the people felt the love in their hearts. As they caressed the soil around the corn seeds they sang, chanting and imagining that these tiny seeds would sustain their tribe forever. Their spirit was resurrected with each harvest.

The yellow corn maiden symbolizes the north, the blue corn maiden speaks for west, red corn maiden represents south, white corn maiden is of the east, the speckled corn maiden stands for the zenith and the black corn maiden for the nadir. In the legend the corn maidens return to chant, dance and sing when the corn is a foot high. In one tale they become the seven stars of the big dipper. Stories create meaning, offer a placement, continuation, history and possibility as well as the integrity of cultural meaning. Dances, songs, drawings and statues to live with as we remember through the richness of the stories that have been recorded and passed on throughout time.

The most powerful teaching tales never take us out of the world but plant us more deeply in it. While often dealing with matters of the spirit, they continually ground us in the facts of daily living, for heaven and earth, nirvana and samsara, this world and the world to come, are simply different ways of experiencing the singular reality of this very moment. And that is what great stories do: they show us a different way to engage reality. Nothing changes but our minds, and this, of course, changes everything.
—Rami Shapiro

We look to the children who are singing and dancing, learning and remembering. Their natural curiosity and interest to learn is noticeable right from birth. What happens as we train and educate with note-taking and testing, isolating the mind to learn science and math in a concrete sequential literal solution-oriented manner? What then happens to creativity and the imagination? When the eagerness to learn is encouraged in its vitality, the enthusiasm for things that matter in life: beauty, sensitivity, love, kindness, as well as the importance of being aware of an inner world of the psyche and the outer world thrive. Young people are inquisitive and alert to learn. Let's cultivate this sense of wonder and enjoyment so it doesn't diminish or wither with aging.

Children are born explorers until they are taught to sit still and obey. —M. Rubin

We live in a world with infinite coastline, can we allow ourselves to stretch into the boundlessness of time, to fathom impermanence so that words overfill their letter. Can we contain *sea* in three letters, *love* in four, *music* in five? We are contained and constrained, conditioned; children are interested in climbing, swimming, playing with butterflies, chasing squirrels, singing, having fun. Their interests are natural. How to preserve this joy, laughter, and song and not divert their energies? How to expand and live open with breadth and depth, into the let's see what wants to happen, passionate and fearless, singing love songs to this universe.

Song of the Sea

Songlines have been a central feature of First Nation cultures for 60,000 years plus. Essentially they are navigational tracks sung to the landscape, used as cues to recall and pass on cultural values and wisdom. This ancient memory code used by indigenous cultures around the world trace the journeys of our ancestors. The miracle of the Native American culture lies in the culture itself, in the garden of their heart which is preserved; in the light-bringers whose generosity of spirit maintains the flame transmitting what has endured.

I like when the music happens like this: Something in His eye grabs hold of a tambourine in me, then I turn and lift a violin in someone else, and they turn, and this turning continues, it has reached you now—isn't that something?
—Rumi

The Dalai Lama, spiritual leader of Tibetan Buddhism, invited Jewish delegates from major branches to travel to Dharamsala, India, where he has been living since 1959 when forced to escape into exile following an invasion and brutal suppression of the Tibetan people from Chinese troops and authority as well as policies that crushed the Tibetan government. The Dalai Lama's inquiry was to learn what has preserved, what keeps the Jewish culture alive.

A unique Buddhist-Jewish dialogue took place; two cultures that have known exile and wandering, and yet have both maintained their identity as a people. Centuries of exile and dispersion for the Jewish people—political repression and denial of the history of Tibetans through Chinese domination—Tibetans face and have also been challenged by serious stressors to their culture and language.

In 1989 after receiving the Nobel Peace Prize the Dalai Lama made a request to the Jewish people: *Tell me your secret, the secret of Jewish spiritual survival while in exile.* Twenty centuries of exile and dispersion, resourcefulness, persistence, resilience, hope, possibility and survival is a trademark for the Jewish people. Heritage encodes us, how does survival when people are scattered all over the world speaking different languages happen? Let us teach what has been the unifying thread, the garments of love that have embodied and carried through generations the spirit of a people.

You may follow one stream. Realize that it leads to the Ocean, but do not mistake the stream for the Ocean.
—Jan-Fishan Khan

As a people of story and the Torah; the sacred text and scripture begin with *once upon a time*. In the first word of the Torah, *in the beginning*, and Jews have been elaborating, telling stories since, creating meaning and purpose. The Jewish people, having been referred to as *people of the stories, people of the book, people of the door* hold the major celebrations in Jewish life to be observed in the home such as the Sabbath, sitting Shiva which is the seven-day mourning period, a mezuzah on a doorpost, the holiday of Passover that encourages children to ask earnest honest questions, holidays that are created as festivities like Purim, chavruta—a fellowship where we gather to share conversations and sit together exploring texts, wisdom study, ancient rituals, narratives that are told at the home table to deepen our connection to the storytelling, music and chants, building a Sukkah to express the impermanence and openness of life, as well as enormous space for disagreement regarding Jewish identity. These challenges have led to conversation, argument, teaching, chanting musical melodies as Torah tropes, study and longevity.

People say stories help you fall asleep, I say that telling stories wakes people up. Every story has something hidden, What is concealed is the hidden light. What was a light that existed before that of the sun? It was a sacred, primordial light, and God hid it for future use. Where was it hidden? In the stories of the Torah…Each story is a crystallization of a greater reality. We take hold of the words and enter into the thought beyond them. —Reb Natan of Bratslav

The world has seen many diaspora populations uprooted, most often it is involuntary, including the removal of Jewish people from Judea, the uprooting/dislocation of Africans through slavery, the exile of Syrians, occupation of Afghanistan, genocide of Armenians and Ukrainians; many people considered to be refugees. Diaspora communities represent and maintain their culture by holding onto the natural essence of the food, costume, holidays, traditional music, rituals, poetry, art and songs of their homeland and childhood.

Every human heart naturally appreciates the beauty of the world. Unravelling the meaning of its songs effectively translates that earthly appreciation into holy words of divine praise. How to train the soul's ear to hear the worlds music on its own accord. The universe sings. Each element brings out a different aspect revealing majesty and flawless benevolence. The songs are constant, filling the heavens and the earth. Even beings that do not have mouths with which to sing express praises of divine beauty with their very existence and natural function. However, the beings can only fully express their messages if we, the conductors, utter their unbroken songs and live according to their meanings. —S. Kraines

Releasing the heart from its cramped container imprints succeeding generations. To reach beyond our ancestors and find our own heartsong and storyline keeps the wheel of life continuously moving. We are all visitors in this guesthouse called the world. Awakening to benefit all human beings here and now we look to our life as an intimate relationship, a partnership with each moment, each activity.

In order for a person to sing, their essential self—heart and soul—must burst into song.
—Piazecyner Rebbe of the Warsaw Ghetto

We recall Miriam, the prophetess, with tambourine in hand—the women followed dancing with timbrels. Miriam was the first woman to be called *prophet, sister of Aaron*, as she led the women—singing, dancing and playing drums. The prophetic nature of music connects us to our own power. Music was an integral part of daily life and the human voice essential as women sang love songs and laments. To step into the biblical period we find a culture filled with music that expressed a variety of moods and feelings; every shade and quality of sentiment are found in the wealth of songs and psalms and in the diverse melodies of the people. Weddings and celebrations were accompanied by music made by women establishing the importance of women's songs. Women's music existed because of the need to compensate for the ban against public participation of women in shared open rituals. It was customary to dance in the vineyards a celebration of joy transforming time into motion.

In order to understand the dance one must be still. And in order to truly understand stillness one must dance.
—Rumi

Women know the secrets of movement, one rhythm—one harmony—one tune; linked to all and everything, pulling back the curtain to see what is revealed. Like the winds circulate fragrances echoing song we experience new creation, training the soul's ear to hear the music, universal praise. We are the conductor of the symphony, each aspect forms our composition. Our entire life is a signature, a love song to creation. What responsibility! Even in the seemingly lifeless desert, winds play music blowing over the sand-dunes, filling the air with sounds as musical instruments.

The great teachers are the songs. How to sweeten our days if not with songs. —Nathan Zach

The Sages taught that song is an indispensable part of our offering. What is our service of joyfulness and goodness of the heart, song. What is it to sing? What is our redemption song? Our timeless anthem, the echos of love and peace. Our mind freed from shackles; this is the emancipation of the mind. And we are all walking, we are walking ourselves and each other home.

Sssh the sea says.   Sssh the small waves at the shore say,

Sssh Not so violent, not so proud, not so remarkable.

Sssh Say the tips of the waves

Crowding around the headland's Surf.

Sssh They say to people, this is our Earth, our eternity.

—Rolf Jacobsen

We are told that Jewish men and women marched into the ovens singing *Ani Ma'amin, I Believe.* A haunting melody transforming hearts from horror into hope, light and promise. This melody on their lips they walked into the gas chambers. To face the unknown, to lift the moment with trust, a vision; present to what is—this is what makes us human.

Remembering, regardless to the circumstances, life becomes the teacher. There is a moment in life when everything comes into focus and makes perfect sense. The incongruities, the pain, hidden messages, all fall into place. In the larger picture a weight is lifted from our shoulders in understanding that things are exactly as they are, and we listen, connect to the breath and sounds of this earth. To open to the heart of the world the invisible becomes visible, a sudden glimpse into what's hidden is our pure moment.

To love a person is to learn the song in their heart and sing it to them when they have forgotten it. —Arne Garborg

The sea is calm tonight off Dover Beach. The birds at dusk cry out syllables of some deconstructed word we are yet unable to decipher to explain existence. And they lift the last light with their wings And fly away with it over the horizon keeping the secret. —Lawrence Ferlinghetti

Emunah

The Invisible

To live the spiritual life is to allow the eternal to manifest in the moment without distorting it with the illusions of what we think it is. —Reshad Field

Emunah is to see the light with our heart when our eyes peer into darkness. Faith as an antidote carries us beyond opening and into a spacious heart of compassion—the vastness of merciful love. Faith in the nature of life becomes a blessing for the next generation. We say amen, emunah—wholehearted affirmation; this is endless love, life itself as an irrevocable condition, home is everywhere. Emunah, trust; we carry the spiritual DNA of the universe. The eye of the heart, our essence lifts a veil to offer a glimpse into the transcendent realm of emunah, fortified through glimpses/tastes of presence. Suffering and joy, hand-in-hand we see with spiritual force and determination and connect to the higher allowing our heart to go where the human mind limits.

Emunah means faith the same root and letters in Hebrew as 'Imun' practice, and 'omanut' art. Faith takes practice. It is an art. —Reb Tirzah Firestone

The stories about hidden treasure become open narratives; legendary quests, their mystical nature are conduits to ultimately reveal light that shines into the dark crevices. Spiritual treasures: faith and truth, yearning and love, oftentimes buried in the heart, simple, ordinary, used to protect and continue ancient sacred mysteries. Heavenly caves are illumined through inner light. Looking beyond form, through it to recognize the jewels inside the seeming emptiness to discover secrets that invisibly surround us. Teachings hidden as treasures have fostered patience as we dive deeper into the unknown mystery. Since all existence is constantly offering teachings, the grasses and trees, the rocks and rivers, each leaf, the stars and sky; we are surrounded, what stands in our way from experiencing the preciousness of life, the vital force of each thing? What a blessing to have this treasured human life. Otherwise it's as if we threw a dazzling diamond into a garbage can, this sacred jewel of human embodiment, of being alive.

Every place the wind carries me is home. —Yu Xuanji

Succinct, once tasting certainty we place ourself in harmonious balance. Perfect surrender. The strength of the invisible carries us knowing that there are worlds and worlds beyond our ability to see, they touch the miraculous. Always here—not always visible to the eye, to look at nature, to hold an inner vision, like being at the helm of a boat during a storm. One hand on the wheel the heart trusting; this is uplifted belief, trust, hope, faith with vision, this wondrous world, true surrender.

♪ *Notes from the Ocean*

Wherever your eyes and arms and heart can move, against the earth and sky, the Beloved has bowed there—Our Beloved has bowed there knowing you were coming.
—Hafiz

According to legend Reb Azriel David Fastag from Warsaw was inspired to hum, to sing as he sat in the cattle car traveling to Treblinka Concentration Camp. He was transformed into a beacon of light, moved by his song the words *Ani ma' amin b'emuna sheleima: I believe with perfect faith.* There, surrounded by hopelessness and suffering, this song of eternal truth, the singing caboose moved along with hundreds of ears and hearts listening, gradually voices raised to join his heart fearlessly, all intertwined. Reb David exhausted and broken open cried out: *I will give half of my portion in Olan Habbah—the world to come—to whomever can bring this song, this hope, to the Modzitzer Rebbe, a song of the eternity of the Jewish people.* This moving song of faith has traveled from Warsaw, Poland, hummed on a cattle car headed to concentration camps, held in memory by a survivor who escaped the cattle car, to Israel and written down then sent onward to New York. Receiving the notes to the song the Rebbe said: *When they sang Ani Ma'amin on the death train, the pillars of the world were shaking. Whenever we sing this we will remember the six million victims and have mercy towards all people.* With this nigun/song on their lips, in their heart, the Jewish people walked to the gas chambers, and today we embrace and sing *Ani Ma'amin* with uplifted heart. Wisdom, understanding and knowledge are the bridge to carry, to practice artful emunah, trust and faith.

A bird gets up every morning and sings its song. It does not wait to hear what other birds are singing, nor does it look to see if another bird is getting more notice. It knows its song innately and sings. This is nature: knowing your song. —Michele Oka Doner

We each carry our unique song, like the writer's voice it has its particular sound. Finding our voice might take many pages/days/years of writing, of practice, until one day we drop/lift into the voice—our recognizable voice and then we are home free. Our natural voice is the instrument we are given and is light itself, once discovered when we notice it dimming we cultivate to invigorate it so as to shine brightly expressing our true spirit. Devotion, openness, responsibility, integrity, clarity, forcefulness; voice is a barometer, evident and indicative, visible to those who pay attention. That's what we love about the great writers, painters, singers, chefs. Their signature which becomes recognizable. We know Shakespeare, we celebrate our familiarity with Picasso, as well as savoring the great chefs trademark dishes. Our inauthenticity self-doubt and judgment mirrors the amount we stray from the essence of who we are. The courage and dedication to the integrity of the moment, to the unseen and invisible holds and carries us forward into the continuous unknown regardless to circumstances. The invitation is always now, we need each moment to recognize the reminders. It's in how we love that offers the opening.

Since it is very rare in our society to be personally sung to, this experience usually awakens the soul and speaks to the heart, helping that person to hear and sing their own song.
—Caitlin Matthews

Silence carries its own trademark tone-sound and has an aliveness, vibration, sensation and we connect through the breath to this rhythmic source, the breath of life. All vibrations have sound hidden within them and appeal or repel us according to the note it strikes in us. To listen, understand and hear silence requires putting aside the furniture and commotion that occupies our mind. This is the peace that passes all thought. Vast and spacious, silence has its own song. Once the noise of the mind, the center of the ego diminishes we trust and surrender, emunah, the invisible manifests to the silent aliveness of life in her fullness in her presence. Worlds within worlds, levels and levels, inconceivable entities, visible and invisible at the same time is the unknown in all of her manifestations. The invisible is as close as our breath. That wordless place where we could meet. Within this mystery, one day to be revealed, messengers we write ourselves into the story, we are here to recount—to tell our story, to speak, to sing, to act on behalf of life, to awaken the heart to the next generation.

Emunah

The music of the night is not in the stars but in the darkness between them. —Homero Aridjis

Our surrender is a stretching, we bend and reach forward—bowing as we lift to the heavens. When we stretch our arms the heart opens. Bearers of love, the quality of our heart radiates from an awareness of the basic simplicity of life. To bring blind faith to conscious faith and experience holiness each moment is the crowning jewel of life. Our actions might not alter the circumstances or events of the day, it's our receptivity and compassion that transforms; as we burn steadily everything becomes our liberation. We are capable of greatness, blossoming; awakening is a work of great love.

So much of the world is plunged in darkness and chaos. So ring the bells that can still ring Forget your perfect offering There is a crack in everything That's how the light gets in. —Leonard Cohen

The sky is a suspended blue ocean, the stars are the fish that swim. The planets are the white whales I sometimes hitch a ride on, And the sun and all light Have forever fused themselves Into my heart and upon my skin. There is only one rule, On this Wild Playground, For every sign Hafiz has ever seen Reads the same. They all say, 'Have fun, my dear; have fun, In the Beloved's Divine Game, O, in the Beloved's Wonderful Game.' —Hafiz

Lamentation from Sorrow to Celebration

Joy, sorrow, tears, lamentation, laughter—to all these music gives voice, but in such a way that we are transported from the world of unrest to a world of peace, and see reality in a new way, as if we were sitting by a mountain lake and contemplating hills and woods and clouds in the tranquil and fathomless water. —Albert Schweitzer

In this life of connection we have moments of forgetfulness. In awareness we remember. We notice, pay attention, learn and transform, uplifting ourselves to the truth of life—everything is connected, is part of the all that is in this life; we take refuge in the collective energy of connection, breathing in awareness we open to stillness, to forget perpetuates suffering. To know; paying attention to human suffering creates a dynamic relationship to mind and body. Nothing achieved, only to be discovered—to re-member, lifting us from forgetfulness to remembrance. The celebration begins the moment we step into the wonder, our love affair with existence; a dance in our heart, to recognize, recall, rejoin with the source of our being. Remembering is to become part of the source again.

Dance, Lalla, with nothing on but air. Sing, Lalla, wearing the sky. Look at this glowing day! What clothes could be so beautiful, or more sacred? —Lalla

Lamentations begin with the Hebrew word *Eicha* —*how*—referred to as the scroll of Eicha, this haunting melody, a song of sorrow expressing life and the light that is the soul dancing. We can choose to join the poets and musicians, the artists that fill the world with song, compositions that are containers for our sorrows. A blessing to find joy in the midst of sadness. How does this happen, this beautiful planet with endless oceans and beauty, and yet? Incomprehension, defiance, outrage, bewilderment; without opening to the incomprehensible, the human experience, our willingness to live with uncertainty and embrace impermanence we would not taste benevolence, hope, kindness and compassion for love to bloom in our broken world. A world we have the opportunity to repair. We witness and testify lifting the veil we are vulnerable, open, humbled. Witness to the suffering of our ancestors we step forward to build a world of, with and for love.

We are created from and with the world To suffer with and from it day by day: Whether we meet in a majestic world of solid measurements or a dream world of swans and gold, we are required to love all homeless objects that require a world. Our claim to own our bodies and our world is our catastrophe. There must be sorrow if there can be love. —W.H. Auden

♪ *Notes from the Ocean*

Our human catastrophe lies in our lack of compassion towards humanity. Creating a communal container we speak as a we, not an I. We regret, we cry. Regret improves our decision making, it deepens meaning. As we violate the universal law of interconnectedness there becomes repetition, that is until we get it right. To live with our sorrows, not be overwhelmed: it's human, and we repair and build, not to discard the broken pieces rather to chisel and be carved and learn from the brokenness. To grieve and become compassionate brings us the power: our greatest regrets might then become our greatest victories. To live, to be lovingkindness; rebuilding this world on kindness we build a world on love. *When I was young I admired clever people. As I grow older, I admire kind people.*

People of our time are losing the power of celebration. Instead of celebrating we seek to be amused or entertained. Celebration is an active state, an act of expressing reverence or appreciation. To be entertained is a passive state—it is to receive pleasure afforded by amusing act or spectacle. Celebration is a confrontation, giving attention to the transcendent meaning of one's actions.
—Abraham Joshua Heschel

Turning, owning our darkness, releasing the form that we pretend we are when the mask becomes the face we turn towards that which remains. Breathing in and breathing out—we are this, committed to a life, to a life of beyond, infinite, welcoming; generosity is our heart's truth. As we open we connect to all humanity, not to be tossed by the waves of anger and remorse, rather to uplift in forgiveness and stand in the truth of this moment. To stand up, to practice, to wake up; one foot in front of another we enter the gateless gate; our initiation into a new way of being.

It's a wonder I haven't abandoned all my ideals, they seem so absurd and impossible to carry out. Yet I keep them, because in spite of everything I still believe that people are really good at heart. I hold my ideals, for perhaps the day will come when I shall be able to carry them out.
— Anne Frank

We grieve and we breathe, from woe to wonder; to embrace death is to embrace life. There is a story about a far-reaching teacher in the history of Tibetan Buddhism, a simple man, Marpa Lotsawa, who worked hard, had a beautiful wife and a firstborn son Dharma Dode, whom he deeply loved. Marpa had a strong spiritual practice and lived mindfully teaching everything he knew and understood to Dharma Dode, his heir.

Marpa had a premonition, telling his son not to attend a festival and not to ride a horse on a particular day, but Dharma Dode did both, was thrown from a startled horse onto a rocky surface and was instantly killed. Marpa felt great sorrow. His students seeing him grieve and having taught them that death was an illusion questioned why he was crying. *Yes, death is an illusion, and the death of one's child is an even greater illusion,* replied Marpa. The pain and tragedies of the relative world are real.

He eventually knew that it was essential to pass his teachings on to others. One day he met Jetsun Milarepa and saw that here was a man who had also deeply grieved, had opened his heart to hardship and yearning. Jetsun had been a murderer. As a young man he became distrustful, angry, resentful, confused and jealous. His father's death, when Jetsun Milarepa was seven years old, was overshadowed by a written will that entrusted the wealth to an aunt and uncle until Milarepa entered adulthood. This aunt and uncle betrayed the heart of the will and Jetsun and his mother were pushed to live in poverty, while the rest of the family lived lavishly from what had been the fathers great wealth.

It was the law of the land that inheritance remained in the hands of the adult male of a family and so his fathers inheritance went to the older brother who sequestered it, and Milarepa and his mother were relegated to live in abject poverty. Violated and watching his mother hungry and impoverished Milarepa became bitter and revengeful. He trained himself in black magic and with this training, pushed also by his mother's desire to punish the relatives, he used what he learned to kill his family. Destroying his uncles house during a festival wedding, thirty-five people, all his relatives, were killed.

Feeling great sorrow, regretting his deeds, remorseful,

Lamentation from Sorrow to Celebration

Milarepa went in search of a teacher to process and hopefully absolve the karma of his past deeds. Milarepa found his way to Marpa Lotsawa and became his student. He was offered the legendary task of building, destroying and rebuilding stone towers, to clear the negativity of his past actions and enter his inward journey. Broken and tired after spending five years in the laborious repetitive task he returned to Marpa and was then sent to train and practice meditation, to live in a cave, to purify his karma from his murderous acts of cruelty, negativity and misdeeds, to open a channel for healing. With heroic effort, dedication, ultimately awakening, he eventually became the psalmist and songster of the Himalayas.

Years of practice, cultivating understanding and forgiveness; his life is an example of struggle, challenge, determination, perseverance and spiritual purification. He uplifted from a life of maliciousness, cruelty and unintended suffering to one of contemplation, expressive creativity, compassion and kindness.

He who avoids misunderstandings, amused at the play of his own mind, is ever joyful. —Milarepa

Jetsun Milarepa is considered to be a great poet-saint. Tibetans accord *The Hundred Thousand Songs of Milarepa* a status similar to the Bible. He is Tibet's Dante, Socrates and Shakespeare. His work is an example of singing dharma, teachings through song. The melodies that Milarepa set his verse to in the twelfth century were popular and known tunes of the day composing his teaching-songs extemporaneously. He practiced and mastered most of the contemplative systems in Tibet at the time and related them through song and verse. Instructive and inspirational teachings offering what it is we create through practice.

I cry, weep and feel a strong sense of faith each time I read or hear the story of Milarepa, the great yogi of Tibet.
—the Dalai Lama

Milarepa's songs of realization are considered to be insightful educational treasures, teaching songs offering reflections and meditations to overcome obstacles. In the singing of his songs we have access and availability to connect to the heart of Milarepa. His colorful and down-to-earth songs, his form of teaching: he traveled about the country expressing spiritual poetry as song, bowing deeply at the altar of praise and blessings.

All meditation must begin with arousing deep compassion. Whatever one does must emerge from an attitude of love and benefiting others, do not entertain hopes for realization, practice all of your life. —Tibet's great yogi, Milarepa

To listen, to hear the inner song of silent spaciousness, to know the harmony of existence through experiencing the melodious beauty of that which is; life is like that, here where we become that, surrendering and penetrating the mystery that is the blessing stream. To put aside the furniture of the mind we look directly into existence with no thing in between, and this is true silence. To listen, to sing our heartsong is key, it's a bridge that connects us to each other. And Milarepa became this; the sacred arose through his presence. Open, existence speaks through us.

However beautiful a song may be, it is just a tune to those who do not understand its meaning. —Milarepa

Milarepa, with persistence and determination innerly traveled from anger to courage, from confusion to clarity. His life demonstrates the possibility of being caught in the mind, creating havoc, negativity and drama, to becoming a student, practicing, owning responsibility, to one day becoming a teacher, a yogi, a priceless repository of enlightened song: awakened, mature, generous and compassionate.

As you embrace the suffering of life, the wonder shows up at the same time. They go together. —Charlotte Joko Beck

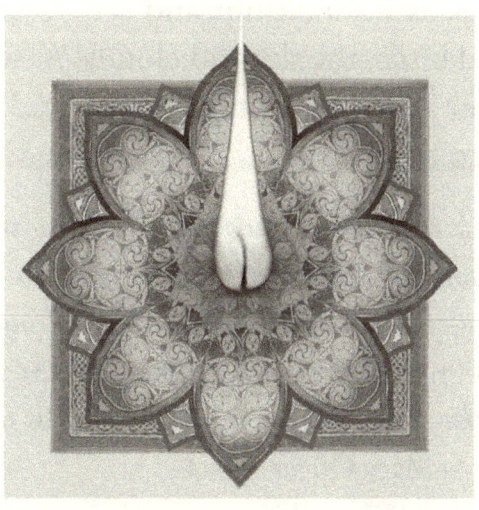

Songs
We are Music!

You must pass your days in song. Let your whole life be a song. —Shirdi Sai Baba

For each of us to discover our own true song, to sing our song; what freedom! To recognize the signature, my voice: this is the invitation, the practice of inquiry. We meet our life most poignantly when challenged, like a diver exploring uncharted terrain, once anchored to our voice we are no longer adrift. Allowing the spark to open us, to penetrate and deepen our understanding, our true nature, to navigate the inner terrain; to listen, hear our voice—We are music! Preparing the soil, creating an environment sets the tone that refines and purifies our energy; we transform opening to the above. The food of the soul is music and song. We hear these inner sounds as we look out and see ocean and lakes, the trees and birds, the sky and clouds. As we polish the rust from our heart, the sounds of love peal out into the air, for life to bloom.

When I walk out into the world, I take no thoughts with me. That's not easy, but you can learn to do it. An empty mind is hungry, so you can look at everything longer, and closer. When you listen with empty ears, you hear more. And this is the core of the secret: Attention is the beginning of devotion. —Mary Oliver

Songs: We are Music

Shir HaShirim The Song of Songs, Canticle of Canticles, this collection of love poetry has been said to be the true basis for all living: love as the all and everything, the inspiration of life itself. This beloved text celebrating joy and goodness is a timeless allegory of the pure expression of love—the erotically human and the divinely inspired. Love is the fount of all relationships. This world is built on/from/for love. This is the nature of life. It is said that human love, which is celebrated in *Song of Songs*, will precede world redemption.

Every Wisdom and Intellect has its own specific tune and melody. —Reb Nachman of Bratislava

We lean to rest upon the wisdom of our foremothers and our forefathers, standing on the shoulders of previous generations to breathe them alive into this present moment. Our thoughts, our heart breathes life into our holy ancestors. This world we might yet build—this unfinished world. As we listen hearing their songs we find meaning and become a blessing to others. This great continuation, even when, even though, is our affirmation, the continuation of human evolution.

Rabbi Zusya used to say: My mother Mirl, peace be with her, did not pray from the book, because she could not read. All she knew was how to sing the blessings. But wherever she sang the blessings in the morning, in that place the radiance of the Divine Presence rested the livelong day.
— Martin Buber

♫ *Notes from the Ocean*

The sanctification of daily life, optimism, hope: the stance, the posture we hold sees light in the darkness. Shifting from sorrow to joy; we swim in an ocean of pain and float in an ocean of love. And now to deepen the companionship, always to ourself and then to the other. *I celebrate myself, and sing myself, and what I assume you shall assume,* wrote Whitman; yes, the two become each other, the two becomes one.

Love is the religion and the universe is the book. Come! Let us choose one another as companions. Let us sit at one another's feet. Come a little closer now, so that we may see each other's faces. Inside we share so many secrets—Do not believe we are simply what these eyes can see. Now we are music together sharing one cup and an armful of roses.
—Rumi

Standing at the shore I have heard *I am afraid to go in the water.* Knowing this life to be risk and consequence, I enter the ocean. Certainly there are no real assurances, only strategy and device—a lifeguard stand, a reading of the tides and ocean conditions, no sea pests rolling onto shore, green flag that signals a non-turbulent water day. This life is similar. Risk and consequence; with what willingness do we drop into sleep at night not knowing if we will awaken? A highway where mindless drivers are, left, right, behind and ahead. Where do I put my thoughts? Unguarded they pass through, uplifted they create space. This beautiful life that holds sorrow and joy. Love and loss. Grief and grace. We sing!

Songs: We are Music

I have used song as the entry and exit point for thoughts. When a thought arrives I have trained myself to turn those words into music and then listen to the message. What is the tune buried deep in my cells telling me? Listening to my inner song unblocks my heart. This world carries the dynamic of trauma, how to connect not to what's wrong with us, to the life force, the animating-spirit to restore what has been untouched and release, unbind the ties to our toxic memories. Leonard Cohen told a friend: *You know, we think we are here to succeed at our given mission. As we get older, we discover that we are here to fail, and not to take it personally.* The depth of that simple statement shifts the music of the heart. And this from the man who ennobled the Hallelujah. Praise the bridge that carries us here; remembering the privilege of aliveness is in the breath of our song.

It is said that before entering the sea a river trembles with fear. She looks back at the path she has traveled, from the peaks of the mountains, the long winding road crossing forests and villages. And in front of her, she sees an ocean so vast that to enter there seems nothing more than to disappear forever. But there is no other way. The river can not go back, Nobody can go back. To go back is impossible in existence. The river needs to take the risk of entering the ocean because only then will fear disappear, because that's where the river will know it's not about disappearing into the ocean, but of becoming the ocean. —Khalil Gibran

♪ *Notes from the Ocean*

Beneath the earth is a seed, when nourished it becomes a song. We water that tender shoot of aliveness with music for the seeds of love to blossom into a flower of love and become a shelter for ourselves and all who want to drink. This bounty of music always available. Is this a song of love, of despair, a childhood ditty, lullaby, anthem, aria, ballad or hymn to remind us of the age of that thought? Now to allow the melody to penetrate and enter the ethers to pass through, one breath, one note at a time.

A miracle, my friend, is an event which creates faith. That is the purpose and nature of miracles. They may seem very wonderful to the people who witness them, and very simple to those who perform them. That does not matter: if they confirm or create faith they are true miracles.
—George Bernard Shaw

What is the melody, the song that is the key to my spiritual survival. The ocean's song. Listen to the song of the sea. To find our theme, our musical melody; for us to marinate so the notes become lodged in cellular memory. To stand in the center of our song; inspired by the mantra of the earth and ocean might become the overture. Melodies are like streams—flowing, we listen to the rhythm, the movement and tempo, to catch the beat the pulse and cadence of life; deep down we know this to be a fluid world. To be alive is to live in a state of constant change, the ebb and the flow, the perpetual rhythm which is a continual movement of what is deepest in ourself. Music reveals the law of harmony, it's a key showing us how to recognize, to find equilibrium; to live in a world constructed of love. Music penetrates deep into our being. Nature reflects that everything is harmonious—trees sway in accordance to the winds and breeze, stars move, the sun rises and sun sets; existence is a great orchestration tuned to the oneness. Let us hear, see, experience living into the harmonic resonance of notes that are life-energy.

Once upon a time there was the simple understanding that to sing at dawn and to sing at dusk was to heal the world through joy. The birds still remember what we have forgotten, that the world is meant to be celebrated.
—Terry Tempest Williams

How incredible to allow our song to emerge, to chant what is in our heart. To listen to our own melody is revolutionary, is what Bob Marley called *Redemption Song. Won't you help to sing these songs of freedom? 'Cause all I ever have, Redemption songs. Redemption songs. Emancipate yourself from mental slavery. None but ourselves can free our minds. How long will they kill our prophets? While we stand aside and look? Won't you help to sing These songs of freedom? Cause all I ever have Redemption Songs.*

Music: What happens when we sing sacred music to the notes of a childhood melody? Like *O Holy Night* to the tune of *Row Row Row Your Boat*. Is this sacrilege, creativity, stretching the boundaries we sing a Christmas tune to a Jewish melody, a Hallelujah at a football game. Roaming through the mind we hum a nigun—a wordless melody, a service of the heart, a prayer expanding our spirit. These wordless songs, a means to elevate the soul, to have fun and move us toward the mystical where life is experienced as unknowable, where life is a song.

In the house of Lovers the music never stops. The walls are made of songs and the floor dances. —Rumi

When the river disappears into the ocean and becomes the ocean; listening to music the words become the sound of the waves, called the sound of one hand clapping. Falling in tune with the music as it takes us to the furthest shore and beyond; such is the nature of song. Love itself becomes the evidence.

Then it shall come to pass, when many evils and troubles are come upon them, that this song shall testify before them as a witness. (Deuteronomy) The suffering and the testimonies, when told by Holocaust survivors, are a song, a hymn of praise, a testimony to the eternity of people and the greatness of their spirit.
—The Rabbi of Bluzhov, Rabbi Israel Spira

The Song of the Universe: Perek Shirah: Songs of Praise, a Chapter of Song, are God's Orchestra. These songs of the universe are constant filling the earth and the heavens. We educate our soul's ear to listen to hear the music of the universe arriving to know creation through her song, the resonant echo of the invisible world. Our very life is our verse: and how we listen is our learning as well as teaching. Helen Keller, without hearing or sight discovered the beauty, listening, hearing Beethoven's *Ode to Joy* through vibrations, listening with her fingers. She was able to recognize human voices, the chorus, feeling with her heart the wonder, the power of music. This transcendent experience, her hand pressed against the radio receiver in her home she heard a live Carnegie Hall broadcast of Beethoven's *Symphony Number 9 in D minor*, composed when Beethoven was himself deaf. She wrote: *what was my amazement to discover that I could feel, not only the vibrations, but also the impassioned rhythm, the throb and the urge of the music! The intertwined and intermingling vibrations from different instruments enchanted me. I could actually distinguish the cornets, the roll of the drums, deep-toned violas and violins singing in the exquisite unison. How the lovely speech of the violins flowed and plowed over the deepest tones of the other instruments…and there I sat, feeling with my hand the magnificent symphony which broke like a sea upon the silent shores of his soul and mine.*

The knower of the generosity of song the deepest mystery of our universe the source of all revelation, this is true freedom. Helen Keller in her unique relationship to song and sound feeling it in her body; listening is a physical experience as we train ourselves to awaken hearing this inner tone. To listen to silence is to be in an interval, in uncluttered spaciousness. To sing and dance, to celebrate as we learn that the body is the guest, the garment; we have access to both, what is called this life as well as the inner continuity that is timeless and eternal.

The Song of the Sea Shirat HaYam also known as *Miriam's Song and the women dancing with their timbrels followed Miriam as she sang her song to the One whom we've exalted, Miriam and the women danced and danced the whole night long.* This song of praise, a unique chant, Miriam the prophet raised her voice in song. This is a departure from other Torah portions, a poem considered to be older than most of the Torah, the language being archaic. *Who among the gods is like you?* Predating monotheism. Mimicking the waves of the sea, a unique chant, Miriam the prophet, timbrel in hand leading women to the sea, singing in celebration, leading in poetic song, a heroic act of faith, redemption, flow of life, and *the women danced the whole night long.*

Song is prayer: what will be our new song, the music when we no longer see separation? Even that the animals and inanimate creations have no mouths with which to sing, their very existence forms a constant song of divine beauty. The stones and clouds and trees and flowers, the mountains and oceans and shells and snails all have distinct melodies. They express their message when we, the conductors utter the verses that sing and live according to their meaning. Hearing the inner music we hear it everywhere, in the stars, in the wind passing through the ocean, in the sound of running water, the shells and turtles, the sands and grass, in the innermost recess of our being there is music. We become song. To live the vision of a harmonious whole soothes the heart. And we are each a unique note in this endless symphony, this soul as sound in a world of endless variety.

I saw you dancing last night on the roof of your house. Whirling beneath the soft bright rose that hung from an invisible stem in the sky. —Hafiz

The solar system with her musical rhythm is a cosmos as is the human body. And the body, like Mother Earth, Mother Ocean, keeps score. Indigenous cultures knew this as they danced and chanted, using ritual and tradition to caretake this holy body, our Earth Mother, Ocean Mother. The musical scale or octave is a universal law that governs the development of all processes in the universe. Understanding the interval, knowing to live into the pause, the gap in between the notes, in the middle of the words, in space, maintains the creative flow of life.

Stories move in circles. They don't move in straight lines. So it helps if you listen in circles. There are stories inside stories and stories between stories, and finding your way through them is as easy and as hard as finding your way home. And part of the finding is the getting lost. And when you're lost, you start to look around and to listen.
—Deena Metzger

♪ *Notes from the Ocean*

A story: A Rebbe would wake up and quietly leave home before dawn each morning to stroll around a nearby pond. In his wisdom and longing he understood and engaged the laws of the universe. Every creature has a song to sing and their melody fills existence in a unique way. So this Rebbe would listen and enter the frog world to learn the chant of the frog, to pray amongst the small creatures. Entering into the music of the frog was the Rebbe's practice—the world of nigunim—the mystical wordless melody, a spiritual language beyond words referred to as the pen of the soul. Sometimes transcending the limitations of words carries great spiritual power.

Music originates from the prophetic spirit, and has the power to elevate one to prophetic inspiration. Song is the soul of the universe. —Nachman of Breslov

What is the Hallelujah, it is our instruction to praise. Earth and heaven are filled with constant music. Every aspect of creation expresses meaning through its song-script. This is the ultimate divine orchestra. Each element expresses herself, fills heaven and earth with continuous song, sometimes happy, some of the time with sorrow. When we hear the melodies, even from beings with no mouth to praise, this great recital: song of the vegetables of the field, the singing of the apple tree and the date palm, the fig tree and the pomegranate, the chanting of the wind and stars and clouds, the birds and sheep and goats, the snail and the ant, all the wonders in this world—a leaf, the dew and the lightening; how do we listen to the musical accolades of existence? How we emulate the sounds as well as the magnificence of the creatures is a testimony to our life. The ocean waves, sea beings, wildlife, fish, plants and trees all have melodic expressive vocal incantations, liturgy that transcend the limitation of language.

There are gates in heaven that cannot be opened except by melody and song.
—Rabbi Shneur Zalman of Liady, founder of Chabad

The writer Y.L. Peretz has written a wonderful story called *The Transmigration of a Melody, A Gilgul fun a nigun*. The story of a wordless melody, a nigun, that wanders from city to town in Eastern Europe. The tune takes on many lives beginning as a wedding song to then become a memorial prayer, an organ grinders song in a circus, sometimes bringing tears to the eyes of those who heard the unspoken music, the wordless notes. The nigun's wanderings continue from home to person to various towns until the melody's migration leaves with one of the song holders who then carries it to America. Spiritual language beyond words; soul expression.

The earth has music for those who listen. —Shakespeare

The story is aptly conveyed in many Leonard Cohen tunes. *Hallelujah* and *Dance Me to the End of Love* were both written in 1984. Hallelujah, from the Hebrew compounded words *hallel* meaning to praise joyously, to express exuberance and *yah*, a shortened form of the name of God, is an instruction from the Old Testament, to sing gratitude, to offer praise to the source of existence. When the Church took on the song in the New Testament as praise, no longer a direction or action it became a synonym for praise the Lord. Beyond religious context, Hallelujah is celebration, sorrow, purification, lamentation, reunion, is an expression of peace. Love will break our hearts, music offers solace: faced with joy and pain, holy or broken, there is always Hallelujah. *And even though it all went wrong, I'll stand before the Lord of Song with nothing on my lips and tongue but Hallelujah.* Leonard renewed the word Hallelujah from a religious word to a secular world. The melody itself with its movement and combination of notes is the blessing. Now a legend, *Hallelujah* is played at weddings, funerals, Friday evening Saturday morning Shabbat services, Christmas mass, American Idol, concerts; a song to comfort, inspire, entertain and beyond all—to welcome. Hallelujah!

Dance Me to the End of Love appears to be a beautiful love song, and, in fact, it was the first dance at my wedding. The lyrics were inspired by the Holocaust. It's curious how songs begin, have their impetus, origination and dawning, *every song, has a kind go grain or seed that somebody hands you, the world hands you and that's why the process is so mysterious—writing a song.* Cohen recalled: *Dance Me to the End of Love came from just hearing or reading or knowing that in the death camps, beside the crematoria, in certain of the death*

Songs: We are Music

camps, a string quartet was pressed into performance while this horror was going on, those were the people whose fate watches horror also. And they would be playing classical music while their fellow prisoners were being killed and burnt. So, that music, 'dance me to your beauty with a burning violin' meaning the beauty there of being the consummation of life, the end of this existence and of the passionate element in that consummation. But, it is the same language that we use for surrender to the beloved, so that the song—it's not important that anybody knows the genesis of It, because if the language comes from that passionate resource, it will be able to embrace all passionate activity.

Each musician would eventually be murdered—enter into the ovens—and this might be the final exultation—the music, the out-breath, the wordless unspoken sound that becomes alive in the music, the dance, to embrace this moment even though we know the inevitable, when the music stops; impermanence, the very nature of life. Yes, eternal love is created from and lives through impermanence, changing form from being to becoming.

You have a song in your heart to be sung and you have a dance to be danced, but the dance is invisible, and the song—even you have not heard it yet. It is deep down hidden in the innermost core of your being; it has to be brought to the surface, it has to be expressed. That's what is meant by self-actualization. —Osho

Part Two

Ocean of Consciousness

Ocean of Consciousness

Acknowledge the wave but stay with the ocean.
—Youngey Mingyur Rinpoche

What is the inner meaning of our life stories? Our obligation, the most difficult, is to love. How to live our birth-right agreements with integrity—offering our life to others in service—comes about from a strong back and soft front. No matter what, to show up in the face of uncertainty, to see things as they are and to remain open, here we are and nothing remains the same. We are called upon to show up and awaken to this life as it is.

When your real, effortless, joyful grateful nature is realized, it will not be inconsistent with the ordinary activities of life. —Ramana Marharshi

We breathe in with the understanding that breath is life. Time as breath, when we breathe we transport consciousness and nourish inner consciousness. This place between heaven and earth is the triumph of our true nature over the sludge of the world with her brokenness—as a fully blossomed lotus, being of light. The Bodhisattva of Compassion, the hearer of the cries of the world, we turn to place attention—our attending to this is our humanity. Yes, we are consciousness!

I wish I could show you, when you are lonely or in darkness, The astonishing light of your own being. —Hafiz

Sh'ma, listen, hear, pay attention! Practice is hearing, listening; that's it. To listen and to love. Our sense of hearing, auditory perception—detecting vibrations, what we experience as the world of sound or neural impulses sent to the brain has been said to be the first that develops in the womb and the final one that leaves as we exit our body. Listen to the song that resonates within you and discover where the sacred and the everyday intersect. The dying brain responds to sound tones even while in an unconscious state. Hearing is the last sense to go in the dying process. Yes, there is a hearer without a hearer.

Sh'ma, Hear. *And you shall love, with a whole heart, with every breath. And these words which I command you this day are upon your heart.* From this ancient 3,000 year old teaching-prayer we ask: Is it possible to command love? As a young person I heard: love your neighbor as yourself, love the stranger. How is it we are to love? In the Sh'ma we are taught that through listening, through being present we awaken love.

The most precious gift you can give to the one you love is your true presence. This is a revolution. If we love someone, we train in deep listening. —Thich Nhat Hahn

Is there a difference between you and I? We become a field of love, capable of real love, our living naturally, open, breathing in whatever arises to dispel the sorrows of this world. We pray our ancestors dreams trusting that what is broken will be repaired. Custodians of hope the promise of yesterday becomes todays world of wonder, the surprise of living, and our life is a responsible voice in the ocean of consciousness, self-evident as light.

Love comes with a knife. You have been walking the ocean's edge, holding up your robes to keep them dry. You must dive naked under and deeper under, a thousand times deeper. Love flows down. —Rumi

It has been said that the state of our mind is what survives from one lifetime to the next. And so the ancient ones cultivated peace of mind, compassion, forgiveness as jewels for this lifetime to address suffering and to cultivate compassion and inner peace. What a beautiful practice. The daily practice of love and compassion begins towards ourself. Love is the foundation of human existence and the basis for inner peace, a bridge between you and all of life. To love we first learn, above all, to be present to our own life.

We have turned our face to the pearl lying on the ocean floor. So why then should we worry if this wobbly old boat keeps going or not? —Hafiz

To integrate the truth of impermanence, the inevitability of death, certainly we might plan for centuries to come, and still not know what will happen in the next moment. Without a question we won't know aliveness, for how can we understand when we don't ask? We distill our experiences after we create a witness, someone home; love is the ingredient. Knowing we are loved is essential and creates presence to teach from our experience. Not to create a copy of ourself—to mend this broken world through our gratitude and appreciation, our service—to face with love impermanence and inevitability, to strengthen our resolve for us to be of benefit to this world, to humanity.

We forget our purpose. All else is distraction, our preoccupation with the trivialities, the nonessential. We are not here to become something. Remember the root of our being, life is for awakening, where the human and the divine meet, this burning of the heart that calls the beloved silently into the night. Forgetfulness of our true nature creates separation. To remember; our witnessing is a compass that brings attention to the moment. Awakening to our true nature we open to the love that always is: greater awareness, a deeper relationship to the inner world, awakened presence. We pause to claim our history, our connections that link the past and future into a freedom called this present moment which carry us into a timelessness called eternity. No longer a trace of me, I am.
—Dr. Paula Bromberg

Questions

Try to love the questions themselves like locked rooms, like books written in a foreign tongue. Live the questions now. Do not strive to uncover answers: they cannot be given you because you have not been able to live them. Perhaps you will then gradually, without noticing it, live along some distant day into the answer. —Rainer Maria Rilke

To live into questions: Who am I? Why am I alive? What is my purpose? What is reality? What is inner work and how do I create that? What is the sound of life laughing, how do I learn to love? What happens when I die? How do I open and continue to remain open in this challenging world? Why is my mind so occupied with thoughts? How to see and respond to conditioned minds? Here we are living in an age of google offering answers—a search away, safety and comfort—for many people a relief. Self-digestion and an honest look at our lies, hypocrisy and willful ignorance, like moonlight reflecting in a hundred rivers false beliefs makes a flaw appear as a virtue. Those who project confidence in good-sounding answers appear as the powerful. Folly masks wisdom. Uncertainty, patience, study, openness, clarity, impermanence, observation, self-inquiry; each an anathema to our current times. We are invited to work on ourself, to become mindful, to self-remember and pay attention, to drop into not knowing, a door opens are we present? What is the sweetness that comes after grief? Listen to questions in search of our loving attentive presence.

Who makes us ignorant? We ourselves. We put our hands over our eyes and weep that it is dark. —Swami Vivekananda

The sage Jiddu Krishnamurti offered a practice: to train ourselves to respond *I don't know* to most questions, regardless to the simplicity or complexity of the question. What will arise when we shake off conditioned habitual ready-made answers and open ourselves to the newness the freshness and truth in this present moment?

There is only one question. And once you know the answer to that question there are no more to ask. That one question is the Original Question. And to that there is only one Final Answer. But between that question and its answer there are innumerable false answers. Out of the depths of unbroken infinity arose the question, who am I?
—Meher Baba

From a very young age Siddhartha Gautama looked into the face of questions: Who am I? What is the meaning and truth of life? As he aged he was aware that the wisdom he was searching for once receiving practices and education and meditating were illusion. We are here to awaken from our illusion of separateness. He moved beyond studies to drop into a silent retreat, releasing formal meditation, eventually answers arrived: there is no answer. And actually there are no questions. Everything is exactly as it is, beyond philosophy, concepts, right or wrong, beyond duality. And with this realization he remained in the forest in seclusion with the understanding that most people are not available to grasp this level of seeing.

Detect a lie and attack the hell out of it. Remember the self-digestion part; this isn't your attack on religion or hypocrisy or any of the ministries, this is your attack on your own willful ignorance. Writing serves as my sword and my torch. It's how I see and how I understand what I'm looking at. —Jed McKenna

It is taught that Buddha offered three teachings: Breath awareness, impermanence, the teaching about our true nature: form is emptiness, emptiness also is form. We are all Buddhas—and in this recognition lies the heart and matter, the essence and precious gift offered over two-thousand-five-hundred years ago. Our place of refuge, a sanctuary. For some the sound of the bell is our invitation to wake up, a moment of presence, a signal that allows us to listen deeply and relax into the present moment. And in this understanding we find true freedom within ourselves. Openness.

Remember that there is no conscious evolution without a pure question. Words are veils over the truth, words are wonderful, as long as the person who is speaking them takes responsibility for the words; to ask a real question may wake us up to be of true knowledge, and to pay for this with our own daily work. Listen first and then you hear. And that is the art of how to ask a question. Life is here to learn by, and this is why the questions are so important. —Reshad Feild

Understanding our birth nature, our naturalness, frees our attention for inner work, magnifies our presence. Within the question there are transformative possibilities; are we available to serve—to live as indistinguishable, invisible from the ordinary person out in the world? The questions that unlock the riches, the treasures, the gold; are we open to listen, to practice compassion in this world, to be discriminating and inclusive? Our expanding awareness, an opening lotus, is to bear witness to the joys and sufferings in this impermanent world, to complete what we have been given, to hear the sound of brokenness and to ask how did this happen? And to not give up on the miraculous.

People say that what we're all seeking is a meaning for life. I think what we're really seeking is an experience of being alive, so that our life experiences on the purely physical plane will have resonance within our innermost being and reality, so that we can actually feel the rapture of being alive. —Joseph Campbell

Remember there are no walls or barriers in love—there is one continuous life and the sound of breath the music of the heart that carries us is to pay homage, bear responsibility; to be living examples witnessing this miraculous experience. The movement and dance of life accompanies us as we proceed up and down the mountain.

There is no present moment without a conscious human being. —Reshad Feild

How to give it away? Energy follows thought as we reach through dimensions. The oceans and stars flow in our veins. The five oceans all are within us. How do we uplift and transform the heart and not spiritualize the ego? Yes, there is a map and it's part of the harmonics of life. Vibration, frequency, sound and tone, water, waves and energy. How to revive what has been buried? The natural movement of life is love, now to untie the knots and arrive into this present moment.

Before his death, Rabbi Zusya said: In the coming world they will not ask me: Why were you not Moses? They will ask me: Why were you not Zusya? —Martin Buber

What is a question? Rarely do we engage that thought. To ask a question from the heart brings about real change. Since all words are our boats, musical notes carry us across and into this lifestream. On our journey ferried with musical notes, an ark we navigate, transported; on our destiny we follow the thread of our life carried by the tides going out and coming in— always a passage of return. When we ask questions what is revealed is about us, the terrain of our mind, about our wonderings. We are the composition, the rhythm, harmony and score: the harmony of life, training to be fully alive—all a precious teaching on the deep natural rhythms of life, death, awakening, and the great beauty and play of becoming and disappearing.

Let me keep my distance, always, from those who think they have the answers. Let me keep company always with

those who say 'Look!' and laugh in astonishment, and bow their heads. —Mary Oliver

We sometimes worry or fret when there is silence, no answer to fill the space of emptiness; coming home to ourselves, present we hear the wondrous sounds of life. Our adult, mature questions enter into us—how to repair this planet that we are given stewardship of? Do we accept the unacceptable? What is friendship and our responsibility towards another? How can I make a healing bridge in this broken world? How to stay open and live compassionately? What practice will support my not being reactive? How to be benevolent and not malevolent? Why is it that to be connected to the higher to what is holy and sacred requires practice? How can I be of use, of service in this lifetime? How to be grateful towards the blessings as well as towards the curses? Questions—we are learning to navigate within this perilous and amazing world. To balance the horror with the wonder.

Letter with question to the Statue of Liberty: Dear Statue of Liberty, Do you like the stairs in your body? What are you reading in that book of yours? —Shayna, third grade

As the child learns through imitation, is nourished by newness and wonder, how do we keep our passion, enthusiasm, questions, curiosity and freshness alive as we walk within this beautiful world of thorns, roses, broken glass, rainbows and surprises?

Questions

Life is routine and routine is a resistance to wonder.
—Abraham Joshua Heschel

Most children have great fun asking seemingly endless questions. But why? the children ask. Why is the sky blue? how far away is the sun? What makes color in the water, how to climb to a star? Why do we bury grandma? What makes the grass green? This wonder and curiosity is less interested in an answer than in entertaining the questions. How to keep these beautiful questions alive and not bound up with adult disinterest and rote platitude solution answers. How to look, listen, breathe, feel our aliveness, freshness and eagerness? Without answers we often feel confused and worried. Beneath each question every answer the child continues to wonder, to look to understand, to feel the magic, to find ways to experience life—the rain, sun, snow, sky, life and death itself. To look through the veils of reality, lifting the curtain of facts and seeing what is underneath, behind; that there is no end to questioning and really no answer to stop the queries. And then how to live in this world when we don't know! How to live an ordinary life in an extraordinary manner. We begin our life with questions and continue throughout our days to discover in awareness that we don't know. The baby dies, a hurricane destroys a community, a shooter enters a school and murders children, a devastating natural disaster—an earthquake in Turkey and Syria killing 40,000 voices, our dog is run over, a tsunami wipes out a small town, six million Jews killed in a Holocaust,

♪ *Notes from the Ocean*

Russia invades the Ukraine, fires spontaneously ignite a local forest; and why?

What if you slept? And what if, in your sleep, you dreamed? And what if, in your dream, you went to heaven and there plucked a strange and beautiful flower? And what if, when you awoke, you had the flower in your hand? Ah, what then? —Samuel Taylor Coleridge

We look to ask so that we open, wonder, raise doubt, be surprised, erase what we imagined and empty out the doctrines, opinions, concepts the conditioning that we once believed. Gone—to live in our experience of life and ultimately to continue to go further, to go beyond.

Growing up turns out to be about suspending questioning, burying it, so that we can get under way with the practical work of getting a living and cooperating with the existing arrangements of the world. Growing up is the submergence of questioning, writes Norman Fischer. *The questioning doesn't go away, still present with us, below the surface, the questioning manifests as anxiety, a vague dissatisfaction with conditions, or loss, or disappointment. Living is questioning and nothing but questioning. Questioning purifies and enlivens everyday life, functioning like a scouring pad or a torch, scrubbing or burning away the patina of desire, confusion, and mindless habit that generally covers ordinary habit that generally covers ordinary activities, so they can't appear as they are; their luminosity is necessarily diminished. With questioning, when we walk we really walk; when we eat we really eat.*

Questions

Nothing false and misleading beyond the moment can withstand the fire of questioning.

To live into the I don't know, that place of openness, free of the madness and thinking is to live in the heart. I look to the ocean and her amazing songs to refresh my heart. What is the source that promotes and extends our aliveness, maintains our attention, creativity, gratitude and astonishment? Certainly to open carries powerful teachings. So a deep bow—thank you for entering/continuing this journey called inquiry—opening and waking up.

The ancient Yiddish question has been: *What makes God laugh? Answer: your plans!*

A prominent Jewish holiday recounts the biblical narrative whereby we see ourselves in each generation as leaving Egypt and moving towards a freedom, a passage from slavery to liberation, from the darkness to the light. Pesach, or Passover, a time of renewal, and since freedom entails a bit of suffering, we recount a narrative that our ancestors restated for 2,000 years. The rituals, celebration and story are here to renew and investigate through questions and discussion.

We are told that the main purpose of recounting the Exodus story is to teach the next generation—and all teaching begins with questions, spoken or unspoken, Questions are what give a teaching its relevance, its grip. —Marcia Falk

We are told of four kinds of children, 4 archetypal

children: the wise one, the wicked, the simple child, and the child who does not know how to ask. We all have the possibility of showing up with aspects of each buried within.

The child's questions, to ask, their sense of wonder and fresh aliveness is paramount to human evolution. The candid relaxed unselfconscious mind manifests an interest in questioning long accepted assumptions, capable of breaking new ground. The power to speak the world into being. To imagine, to dream—the questions asked create a new world. Radical uncertainty, our invitation, nourishment for the soul. Lean into love—what else is there to do? Who am I in this world? Robust uncomfortable conversations assist to maintain our connection to our inner life. In a world deprived of compassion we have an obligation to practice loving-kindness. Unfamiliar, uncertain, how to live into the everything is new? Things being what they are allow us our immediate connection. Self-inquiry—the risk and sacrifice: those who have a *why* to live can bear with almost any *how*.

I am happy before I have a reason. I am full of light even before the sky can greet the sun or the moon. Dear companions, we have been in love with God for so very very long. What can Hafiz now do but forever dance!
—Hafiz

The questions disappear as they are lived, experienced. This is true nourishment, feeding the deepest part we become the question—when not addressed we diminish intimacy. Our questions are there to disturb, they are here looking for truth. The answer lies in our experience of silence, of appreciation and openness, of allowing the *because* to sink deeply in, to the but *why?* What is underneath the facts, our bridge to the unknown, to the hidden mystery the continuation of this unfolding—poetry in the making. Authentic questions arise from true interest, from a place of surprise, our *Leela*—a playful dance: our presence is the answer. How we walk, talk, move, behave, dream, respond. There are questions that open a door to a fresh new look at the world.

If tomorrow morning the sky falls have clouds for breakfast. If night falls use stars for streetlights. If the moon gets stuck in a tree cover the hole in the sky with a strawberry. If you're afraid of the dark remember the night rainbow.
—Cooper Edens

In our readiness are we penetrated? Questions are not only curiosity and self-importance; this is about lifting our being. What does it mean to live in the gap, in the spacious emptiness that holds the question? Until absorbed, lifting our being? Our wholeness lies in our response to above and below: between the pull of this earth and the people here as well as a call from celestial realms. Receptive, we enter to deepen our connection, our sense of wonder and surprise.

♪ *Notes from the Ocean*

It is the nature of the world of form that nothing stays fixed for very long—and so it starts to fall apart again. Forms dissolve; new forms arise. Watch the clouds. They will teach you about the world of form. —Eckhart Tolle

Eventually all questions are reduced to the essential question, who am I? How am I? Inquiry into our great questions that transform in time as we roam about in this continuously evolving universe, as we journey in the seas of time, sometimes walking in the shallow waters, other times diving deeper into the ocean, and always to new beginnings, to live in this paradise we know as home, even though; and we live keeping our questions alive, who am I? Are we entering the door asking, what is a real question and how can I live into that mystery of silence and of not knowing? How to deepen the questions ultimately understanding that there are no answers. Here we are experiencing, tasting, digesting our life.

I remember preparing to interview Ganga-ji and on another occasion Elie Wiesel. I arrived ready to engage in conversation and my mind stopped. There I was open, vulnerable, speechless, without a thought or question, sitting in presence. Open to be. Still. Soul talk. How to give voice to the light, to the conversation between nightingales and flowers, we sit together smiling. Rumi wrote: *The core of the seen and unseen universe smiles, but remember smiles come best from those who weep. Lightening, then the rain-laughter. Love is* that. No expectation only surprises this love. And our presence is the answer to absorb.

In this universe we are given two gifts: the ability to love, and the ability to ask questions. Which are, at the same time, the fires that warm us and the fires that scorch us.
—Mary Oliver

I remember each day walking into class with the assignment to write a real question. And Reshad, my teacher, would stand reading each index card and say *that's not a real question* until he found what he named an *honest question*. How do we find the question in our heart? And most important—how to keep our questions alive.

The beautiful poet Rilke wrote: *Be patient toward all that is unsolved in your heart and to try to love the questions themselves like locked rooms and like books that are written in a very foreign tongue. Do not now seek the answers, which cannot be given you because you would not be able to live them. And the point is, to live everything. Live the questions now. Perhaps you will then gradually, without noticing it, live along some distant day into the answer.*

The questions themselves are holy to savor and allow our imagination to freely explore, how we see life changes the way life appears. Children unselfconsciously ask. Our answers either limit or expand their playfulness. And there is only this present moment, fresh vibrant, light. Life is never safe, there is always risk; the question is, how much discomfort are we willing to live within? There is no birth without a journey and within this unpredictable world for us to remain vulnerable, open to the needs of the moment, we allow the changes that authorize us to be a servant of existence. The material of our life is our life. Paying attention, embracing everything, to sanctify life in the face of impermanence we become human.

What makes a human being is the capacity of his/her questioning. Asking, Who am I? Is the most absorbing question that a human being can have. To know what we are here for. Who are we? —William Segal

There is a rich teaching story in the Mahabharata, the ancient Indian epic. Five brothers, each one an exiled prince, wandered into a forest wilderness without food or water. Coming upon a lake a beautiful crane was standing at the boundary of the water and spoke: *Stop! This is my lake and if you bend to drink the water before answering my question you will die.* The first four brothers ignoring the warning, bending to drink immediately fall dead along the lake's edge. The fifth brother, seeing this display, struck by what he saw, now grieving for his four dead brothers, agrees to listen for the question. Open to surrender beyond his thirst to hear and to pay attention to the crane. *What is the most astonishing thing in life*, asks the crane? The oldest prince paused and then replies: *While we see and hear that people are dying we almost never imagine that we too will one day die.* The crane, surprised and satisfied with the clarity depth and truth-telling of the fifth prince now reveals himself to be the god Dharma—the one who rules over our life purpose, our true calling, what we are put here to do. Dharma restores the four brothers to life, saying: *truth is a great testimony, a precious gift. Thank you. It shapes the tongue into Love, turning sorrow right side up.*

Love is the answer whatever the question.

Love is the answer, and you know that for sure; Love is a flower, you've got to let it grow. —John Lennon

Deep Listening

I suspect that the most basic and powerful way to connect with another person is to listen. Just listen. Perhaps the most important thing we ever give each other is our attention.
—Rachel Naomi Remen

As we learn to live within the rhythm of life, cultivating attentive listening is prayer. Praying is paying attention to this universe, not only to hear ourselves, it's to hear the sounds and songs of life. Listening to our own music is a practice that takes us home, a practice that is available to us in joyful times as well as in difficult moments. Going into surgery, at the dental office, driving in traffic, waking up to the melodic notes of the birds, visiting a hospital hearing ventilators, walking within the music of leaves rustling, paying attention to the resonant sound of our breathing; it's revolutionary, it's a healing strategy to fill our tool kit—a preparation for all occasions.

Once upon a time, when women were birds, there was a simple understanding that to sing at dawn and to sing at dusk was to heal the world through joy. The birds still remember what we have forgotten, that the world is meant to be celebrated. I pray to the birds because they remind me of what I love rather than what I fear. And at the end of my prayers, they teach me how to listen.
—Terry Tempest Williams

Deep Listening

My repertoire is whatever appears in mind. From toddler/baby music to Gregorian chants, gospel, opera, Hebrew and Yiddish song, blues and jazz. From a place of inner quiet music arises. From a place of inner duress I choose to allow a song or notes, a chant or musical instrument to enter my head space, to quiet voices noise and chatter that arrive into mind and occupy thought space. Opening to a larger vision, a greater experience of life—to live in the present moment is so radically simple.

I woke up this morning and I felt grateful to be alive. I watched the sun rise, like it normally does; there's no problem for the sun. I heard the birds singing as they normally do; nothing is out of place for the birds. I saw the trees and flowers budding for Spring as they usually do; everything is perfectly in place for the trees and flowers. And then I wondered whether nature is trying to tell us something. Do not worry, all is well, everything is fine. Shine, sing, be happy! —Rhonda Byrne

This is the earth's pulse, sound waves ocean waves, each bring melody. Sometimes gently, rhythmically chanting a word like *Hallelujah,* or *Om Namah Shivaya* carries me into the melodious movement of a running brook, of a bird warbling, humming, dancing, hearing the beat of my heart; powerful prayers to the heavens. Doors open—this and more are the songs of the universe. Since all language, all creation is music, when we listen we are opening doors to allow ourselves to be penetrated by musical vibrations.

♪ *Notes from the Ocean*

When I was young enough to still spend a long time buttoning my shoes in the morning, I'd listen toward the hall: Daddy upstairs was shaving in the bathroom and Mother downstairs was frying the bacon. They would begin whistling back and forth to each other up and down the stairwell. My father would whistle his phrase, my mother would try to whistle, then hum hers back. It was their duet. I drew my buttonhook in and out and listened to it—I knew it was 'The Merry Widow.' The difference was, their song almost floated with laughter: How different from the record, which growled from the beginning, as if the Victrola were only slowly being wound up. They kept it running between them, up and down the stairs where I was now just about ready to run clattering down and show them my shoes. —Eudora Welty

Listening to this moment, to hear it's directive, there is a rhythm that is a continuous unfolding, now to live within the mystery in heightened sensitivity to life. The way appears as we listen: to ourself, to the other; listening deeply darkness turns into light, the ocean waves disappear and what's left is the sea. Everything speaks, has its personal language: each stone, fruit, piece of wood, pot of paint—and in this life to pay attention as a master craftsperson we assemble, allow the creation of its language to come forth. This is art: a conversation with the wood, the stone, fabric, the air, our body, the insects and wind, the animals inside and out, the foods we cook. They speak, we listen.

Deep Listening

To listen deeply within is to awaken the musician.
—Don G. Campbell

Listening is a love affair, it's magical and miraculous. When every fiber of our being listens, through our ears, our feet, hands, heart, we meet and disappear. Cultivating a listening heart is a practice. Children and adults yearn to be seen and heard. How many times have we seen a young child tugging at adults to be listened to—while the adult is chatting with a friend, looking on their digital equipment, busy with something and not present to the child. Oh, to be listened to, to receive full attention, a primal need rarely filled.

You know, people come to therapy really for a blessing. Not so much to fix what's broken, but to get what's broken blessed. —James Hillman

Sh'ma, listen, a directive! A powerful call that brings us to an action; until we place the words of our heart into love through understanding—then, when that transforms our life we listen and remember; this force that connects us leads to oneness. True listening asks us to open, for heart to touch heart. This is the I-thou relationship, to loosen, to remove barriers. Listening is key. When you listen, truly listen!

The Sh'ma directs us to go further, to listen and to love. Compelling and complete this simple instruction, and when we chip away we are home—to listen and to love, and listening is deep love. We practice so that each moment of our life we are alive. When we listen to someone, to really listen. And the world appears more beautiful, even still.

Listen, listen, this wonderful sound of the bell brings me back to my true self. When we listen deeply it helps us to wake up. —Thich Nhat Hahn

To remember—begin with listening, this deepens our capacity to love—building bridges not barriers to touch the oneness. Deep listening creates a space to ease the suffering of others and to mindfully hear the needs of our earth and ocean. Training ourself to listen with compassion opens the heart. Alert, silent, open, receptive, present to the sound, the rhythm and tone, a door opens for us to live harmoniously. I have spent many years listening feeling the nature and heart of the person through their voice, their tone and cadence, through the telephone line, without seeing the visual of the person. Voice is breath and each voice expresses its value and essence. To deeply listen we hear beyond the words what is behind the words, to encourage an enlivened life-force. This is our living breathing: to be present through time and space.

I am a hole in a flute that the Christ's breath moves through—Listen to this music. —Hafiz

Understanding

Understanding is the only discipline. Understand your activities and suddenly, in the middle of the activity, if you become aware, it will stop. If you become aware why you are doing it, it will stop. And that stopping is what Tilopa means 'Do nought with the body but relax.' —Osho

What we want, how we live arises from our capacity for understanding. We are our understanding and out of that emerges what we want. A demand for understanding is the principal claim made upon us, the most powerful strongest force. The subtitle for my previous book was *The Way of the Lover A Way of Understanding The Fifth Way-Life at its Best*. As the book evolved I recognized that self-understanding is the entrance way, a door we enter to bring us to the threshold of a spiritual life. Self-Understanding is the beginning of wisdom, and this implies spaciousness, emptiness, a silence which includes the energy of the universe. Once we establish communication within ourself we learn how we approach life, then understanding arises. Can we look at ourself with all of our senses and free of conditioned opinions?

Learning our nature—we each have a particular nature—looking at our traumas, and we all have had at least one—is the groundwork for the larger world of understanding. Our collective trauma as well as our personal legacies contain the seeds to bloom into a healing for our planet. There can be no authentic understanding without the initial work of self-understanding, otherwise we become spinning wheels, conceptualizing intellectually, building our world on a shaky foundation. Our recognition, self-awareness is what allows decisions to develop as we are rather than embellishing fantasies and fascination. Sounds so simple, our movement towards maturity. This includes investigation of the strategies that we chose, oftentimes called addictions or identification, which we all have; addicted to escaping reality, and now, do they serve our higher purpose or are they currently impeding our movement towards maturity. Bowing to the mystery we become witness to the wealth, the treasure, to the greatness of life.

I want a man to reach a stage of understanding so that he can be bent, twisted and turned and yet he will always point in the same direction. —G.I. Gurdjieff

Knowing the strategy we picked to keep us in the game, rather than killing ourself, to protect our life—that is our essential significant life-learning discovery. We all chose some tactic to guard the preciousness that is inherent. Some choose defiance, arrogance, self-deception, defensiveness, money, work, aggression, worry and hurry, exercise, watching television, some have picked alcohol, food or sex, marijuana or arguing, travel and adventures, isolation or sequential partners; whatever the choosing it most likely is now our obstruction. We stand in our own way. We have fed the wolf to preserve the lamb, savored the lie, the illusion over the truth, yet without true understanding of our strategy and the courage to dismantle it we are missing the sacred holiness of life. Simple it might be to change the objects of our cherishing, to look deeper at what we have put in the way of waking up. What maintains the distress, the unhappiness and unnecessary suffering? With understanding we can ease to drop the self-deception and illusions. One breath at a time. The courage to be real. Training ourselves to see the hidden, to live in universal being as metaphor for our inner life, we learn to listen, for clarity. From the challenges and stumbling, the remorse and regrets, the hope and beauty our understanding arises.

Your understanding of your inner self holds the meaning of your life. —Leo Tolstoy

To live in the rhythm of life, in loving listening, in understanding the tone of our life, we are bathed in sound, frequency and vibration. We are the instrument with a possibility of restoring ourselves and the planet to a harmonious balance. Throughout our life we are borrowing and taking in energy from the external world. The conscious transformation of energy means that we are no longer at the mercy of what comes our way, or as one spiritual teaching said: *without understanding energy we are just waiting for roast pigeon to fly into our mouths.*

♪ *Notes from the Ocean*

Writers are great lovers. They fall in love with other writers. That's how they learn to write. They take on a writer, read everything by him or her, read it over again until they understand how the writer moves, pauses, and sees. That's what being a lover is: stepping out of yourself, stepping into someone else's skin. We are important and our lives are important, magnificent really, and their details are worthy to be recorded. This is how writers must think, this is how we must sit down with pen in hand. We are here; we are human beings; this is how we lived. Let it be known, the earth passed before us. Our details are important. Otherwise, if they are not, we can drop a bomb and it doesn't matter. Recording the details of our lives is a stance against bombs with their mass ability to kill, against too much speed and efficiency. A writer must say yes to life, to all of life. Our task is to say a holy yes to the real things of our life as they exist—the real truth to who we are. —Natalie Goldberg

Through our words and actions we bring love into the world. Love without knowledge, without consciousness, without knowing what love is and how to love is the appearance. For love to flow through and take hold of the world there must be understanding. Self-love is the beginning. Surely it cannot end there, for without further investigation and growth our traditional customary sentimental, self-important love impedes human society; the ego loves nothing higher than itself. Consciousness and awakening are higher than self-love. For love to become more than a veiled extension of self-love it has to become conscious love, an art that requires self-discipline and self-education.

The gods love each other consciously. Conscious lovers become gods. Without shame people will boast that they have loved, do love or hope to love. As if love were enough to cover any multitude of sins. Love, when it is not conscious love—that is to say love that aims to be both wise and able in the service of its object—is either an affinity or a dis-affinity, and in both cases equally unconscious, that is uncontrolled. Until you have wisdom and power equal to your love, be ashamed to avow that you are in love. Neither the purpose or the function of conscious love is children. Take hold tightly; let go lightly. This is one of the great secrets of felicity in love. Great love can both let go and take hold. —A.R. Orage

The scab that covers our woundedness, that has protected us has many disguises. To bow down and challenge these distractions; they are at the heart of our dysfunction and unnecessary suffering—tenderly understanding them arms us, frees us. How to live in this world without the armor, without being walled in behind a defensive posture of self-involvement, self-importance and illusion? To understand and dissolve our strategies—the ones that impede true joy and love, inner peace and happiness, the ones that stand in the way of having a deep connection to ourself and others is our practice before they become permanent landmarks that lodge in our physical body. To study and understand, to risk not being enticed by the opinions of others, to dare to look with relentless honesty is our journey towards wholeness.

Dysfunctional families tend to cater to the most toxic person. The other family members do everything in their power to keep the toxic person happy. —Laura K. Connell

Understanding grows out of experience, meeting the universe from the inside it wells up within, grows from us, is ultimately liberating. First listen, then open, now understand. Touching the miraculous we wake up out of the dream of separation. Taking responsibility is to offer ourselves to what is happening; it's risk, pledging ourselves to our life, showing up. This visibility and willingness emanates from understanding beyond the rational—sometimes we do things that are a challenge to rid ourself of the toxicity of this world. Cultivating compassion to bless our broken places and embrace/enjoy who we are: from the heart we touch the invisible. Until we become understanding, no separation, an expansion arrives that is beyond understanding, a spontaneity without words, this rhythm of the universe where life continues and we celebrate.

When we want to understand something, we cannot just stand outside and observe it. We have to enter deeply into it and be one with it in order to really understand. If we want to understand a person, we have to feel their feelings, suffer their sufferings, and enjoy their joy. Love is impossible without understanding. Understanding

Understanding

is the fruit of meditation. Understanding is the basis for everything, no understanding, then no attainment. Understanding is the essence of a Buddha. You cannot love someone if you do not understand him or her. If you don't understand and you love, that is not love; it is something else. Without understanding, love can't be true love. Perfect understanding is the destroyer of all suffering, the highest, the unequalled mantra. We must look deeply in order to see and understand the needs, aspirations, and suffering of the ones we love. —Thich Nhat Hahn

Love deepens with understanding the interrelatedness of all people. To see another, this beautiful encounter of understanding creates friendship. Now we are able to offer intentional understanding to what the other prefers, what is needed. When giving is from the root of our being we practice loving regardless to our hurts, resistance and intellectual activities. No holding back, what we resist persists, and so to remain the openness we are leaves us free to enjoy and know intimate partnership. Seeking understanding; a spiritual pull creates distance from the emotional upheavals that toxify relationships. As false personality diminishes and we place attention on mindfulness the ordinary is experienced as remarkable. This nature is how we are. The individuality and unorthodox lifestyle, rarely doing what is not heartfelt, creates inner dialogue and a substance called self-worth. Love pursued, this is the step of realizing that the source of love is internal and the desire for union becomes the spirit of truth.

♪ *Notes from the Ocean*

The forest was shrinking but the trees kept voting for the axe, for the axe was clever and convinced the trees that because his handle was made of wood he was one of them.
—Turkish proverb

When we imagine understanding while disagreeing with another we deceive ourselves; understanding the other we are in agreement, and when we disagree we are not understanding. Understanding is the most powerful force that we create in ourselves—it brings about internal spaciousness. Deep within ourselves is a voice, self-awareness blossoms listening, following the sound to its original longing. Benevolence is always moving towards us. Learn to open the dam, to release the waters, to allow love to flow; stagnant water is not inviting, flowing water remains fresh. To acknowledge and recognize ourself in another births a love that understands the oneness, eliminating separation. Love is not other than yourself, no one is left out. It arises as our natural being when the obstacles that impede its flowering are surmounted. The duality of lover and beloved cultivates illusory separation. Maintaining this illusion restricts us from love's reflection, from love's oneness. This at-one-ment is being in tune, in harmony with the whole universe.

The moon and sun are eternal travelers. Even the years wander on. A lifetime adrift in a boat or in old age leading a tired horse into the years, every day is a journey, and the journey itself is home. —Basho

Suffering

A person who is beginning to sense the suffering of life is, at the same time, beginning to awaken to deeper realities, truer realities. For suffering smashes to pieces the complacency of our normal fictions about reality, and forces us to come alive in a special sense—to see carefully, to feel deeply, to touch ourselves and our worlds in ways we have heretofore avoided. —Ken Wilber

Suffering, we bear the unknowable, surrendering to life as it appears. Embracing our human heartache, not turning away we dwell in the mystery, the paradox, unmasking our illusions, present to the miracle of being alive. Our attitude toward circumstances and not the particular event determines the suffering. How to maintain balance and grow through suffering?

Suffering has a redeeming quality. Pain and repetition are fixative agents. The reader will find it very repetitive. Naturally so. For it is the story of a teaching. And teaching is constant repetition. The pupil has to learn the lesson again and again in order to be able to master it, and the teacher must repeat the lesson, present it in a different light, sometimes in a different form, so that the pupil could understand and remember. 'If you want Truth as badly as a drowning man wants air, you will realize it in a split-second.' But who wants Truth as badly as that? It is the task of the Teacher to set the heart aflame with the unquenchable flame of longing, and it is his duty to keep it burning till it is reduced to ashes. For only a heart which has burned itself empty is capable of love. Only a heart which has become non-existent can resurrect, pulsate to the rhythm of a new life. 'we are both the Pilgrim and the Way.' —Irina Tweedie

We have a choice—to be present with our challenges transforming energy, ultimately to be less affected by whatever appears. Energy is life manifesting as pulsating expansion and contraction. To re-establish the balance between ourselves and the world, understanding our placement within this cosmos. Rumi describes this movement: *Your hand opens and closes and opens and closes. If it were always a fist or always stretched open, you would be paralyzed. Your deepest presence is in every small contracting and expanding. The two as beautifully balanced and coordinated as birdsongs.* The pulsating energy we call life is rhythm, the pacing of contraction and expansion, a dance of joy and suffering. The breath and heartbeat, ebb and flow, internal and external are stages of growth, evolution and possibility.

If we are asleep we cannot see the purpose in life, and thus cannot see the purpose of suffering. —Reshad Field

How can I use this suffering? Inevitably pain arises. The path through suffering is having resources and tools to hold onto while we walk through this world, gradually the pain diminishes to see this beautiful life as it is.

Suffering

Fourth Way teacher Gurdjieff taught that there are *two kinds of suffering—conscious and unconscious*. And stated that *Only a fool suffers unconsciously, useless because it is accidental, almost always harmful*. When our life is permeated with involuntary unnecessary suffering it's difficult to regard any challenge as positive. Life becomes focused on escaping and avoiding discomfort, our mechanical automatic reaction. Voluntary suffering contains a purification. No real/intentional suffering is wasted, it's a payment: now not to suffer more than is necessary. The temporary friction of owning each experience—turning the moment towards good use creates/builds inner substance. Eventually hard times pass and new possibilities appear.

People suffer mechanically. It is something quite different from conscious suffering. Mechanical suffering so contradictory, so long-standing, a habit. Life is a pain factory. To give up our mechanical suffering we have to be able to see what we suffer from and not justify it.
—Maurice Nicoll

There are different forms of suffering: physical, emotional, intentional, voluntary, real/necessary and unnecessary. Real or necessary suffering is physical pain, emotional suffering might be the death of a child. Unnecessary suffering is our unreasonable attitudes and expectations towards others from our ego and vanity. Unavoidable heartbreak arrives through accidents or events beyond our control—like war, disease, disaster or death. Voluntary suffering are projects we agree to in order to follow an aim: like a student who works to have good grades for a college admission or athletes disciplining themselves to win an olympic medal. Awakening our conscience is taking responsibility for our thoughts and actions. To be resilient and in charge of our life, not reacting when someone *steps on our corns*, loosening the comfortable routines of our life, looking at our fears, self-pity and resentments; as we loosen the comforts and continue to see the mechanicalness of our habits we open space for higher forces, for love to enter. Guided by sustained intention creates clarity, transforming/freeing our inner mental state away from unnecessary suffering.

Trying to avoid suffering is suffering. We have been trained and conditioned to steer clear of pain through medication and distraction. Intentional suffering is the deliberate purposeful acceptance of all suffering which is the true nature of existence.

Buddha and bodhisattvas suffer too. The difference between them and us is that they know how to transform their suffering into joy and like good organic gardeners, they do not discriminate in favor of the flowers or against the garbage. They know how to transform garbage into flowers. Don't throw away your suffering.
—Thich Nhat Hahn

Suffering is an elemental ingredient of life. Once we accept the difficult we are walking along a path freeing ourselves from Maya's house of mirrors, the shadow of images where there are no originals. How to transform ourselves into a joyful open loving mature adult? Openness, gratitude, happiness determined by our state of mind is the path. For many people happiness exists in self-indulgent gratification/pleasure, mostly through bodily sensations of food and sex, quantity and sensations, often superficial. Mechanical, our immature emotional life encourages habits of permissive extravagance, busyness excessive unrestrained unfocused distractions. Much of our conditioned life avoids going inside, deeper where inner self-study originates.

If you watch your life carefully you will discover quite soon that we hardly ever live from within outwards; instead we respond to incitement, to excitement. In other words, we live by reflection, by reaction. Can we live simply by means of the depth and the richness within ourselves?
—Anthony Bloom

How to live in happiness, regardless to what is out there in the world, knowing that the mind component creates or blocks happiness? This world thrives from our happiness. How to be present to the simple wonder and beauty in the moment? It's mind-boggling that we have to learn to be present! Now to be in the midst of life and remain peaceful in the heart.

The resistance to the unpleasant situation is the root of suffering. —Ram Dass

To look more deeply at ourselves and learn to develop inner work, rather than what Gurdjieff called *stupid suffering*, self-appointed misery; rather to become present and live into our experiences. How can we use our hardships rather than be used by them? What is the transformation of suffering? How can we benefit from our suffering rather than languish in vain? Then we know how to use our life to lift ourselves as well as to serve others.

You wish to know 'why we are born and why do we die?' To really know you must suffer. You must learn to suffer not as you do now, but consciously. We are to hurdle the difficulties holding fast to our aim in spite of everything.
—Gurdjieff

Jean-Paul Sartre wrote a short one-act play around this theme named *No Exit*, based on his observation: *hell is other people*. The original title is the French translation of the term *huis close, with closed doors, in private*, an idiomatic French expression—no one leaves or enters—*No Exit*. To Sartre what restricts us, our personal life, is being condemned to an eternity of torturing ourselves and each other without an exit. Trapped in the struggle which continues interminably, no resolution, only continuation. Even when the door in hell swings open there is no exit for these tragic beings. There is no longer the freedom to change, to shape life, to correct what is seen or convert and inspire the past.

Tasting the bitter with the sweet, recognizing the difference between pain that is hurtful and pain that changes us—awakening to our true nature, every scar; each trauma holds a lifetime of opportunities, an endless array of teachings. Sartre's work demonstrates the devouring gaze of the other, the negative manifestations of others, how we allow that to restrict our freedom, played out on the stage through the eyes of audience members.

Suffering shows where you are attached, when it arrives, it certainly turns out to be grace. —Ram Dass

Hell, like war, is other people. We get mired down in outside opinions and judgments. The characters in *No Exit* torture each other. This intense and compressed dramatic parable, mirroring life, presents a core existential truth: each individual ultimately faces self-truth and consequence, forced to an inescapable encounter with others who without being invited in offer polarizing platitudes from their level of perception, a subjective measure of moral ineptitude.

To be surrounded by the ceaseless concern of judgments and actions, can we break out of the circle of hell that is other people as well as our inner chatter? Self-deception; there are no mirrors in the room, rather we are seen by the other and can't avoid one another's gaze nor escape our own and other's judgments and dehumanizing stare. This vehicle tries to make sense of the moral and metaphysical implications of war and humanity exploring relationships and our human condition.

A writer's work is to name the unnameable, to point at frauds, shape the world, and stop it from going to sleep. A poem cannot stop a bullet. A novel can't diffuse a bomb, but we are not helpless. We can sing the truth and name the liars. We must tell better stories than the tyrants.
—Salman Rushdie

Everything in this universe goes through a state of distress or hardship. Part of the training towards maturity includes suffering with the understanding that things are complementary, not opposite. To know joy we also know sorrow. This world exists for us to taste, and we learn this until through experiencing compassion our understanding arises. Leonard Cohen wrote and sang *Now I greet you from the other side of sorrow and despair, with a love so vast and so shattered, it will reach you everywhere.* This profound song offers a hand of kindness, *Even though it all went wrong I stand right here before the Lord of Song with nothing on my tongue but Hallelujah.* Yes, we can find love in this broken world. *There is a crack, a crack in everything, that's how the light gets in.* We find love and redemption, a chink, a gap—an opening—pointing towards possibilities in the darkness. *Ring the bells that still can ring.* Leonard wrote that there *is no excuse for an abdication of your own personal responsibilities toward yourself and your job and your love. Ring the bells that still can ring: they're few and far between but you can find them.* Our looking more deeply into the darkness is where we find the courage and strength to sing. This is where transcendence, transformation is discovered: to understand and interpret suffering into a wider context. This marriage of the sacred and the profane, where we are imperfectly perfect, yes, there are flaws, and there is hope. Cracks in our political systems, our economic and social structures, ecological darkness. And yet, this opportunity—the light that arrives through the cracks offer us choice and purpose. We are one world—pandemics and environmental crisis point to this. The fractures and disruption direct us, point to engaging, to becoming that light. *You want it darker,* sang Leonard, *Hineni, here I am*! Showing up—both a surrender and a behold—look what I am pointing at for us to embrace.

I saw grief drinking a cup of sorrow. It's sweet, isn't it? Grief said, You put me out of business. How can I sell grief when you know it's sweet? —Rumi

Taking responsibility is showing up, even though, regardless to the consequences we stand for our values, to be liberated from our past, face our grief, not look away, to show up. Our suffering can inform our lives. We vote because we see this as an earned privilege, we are not in control, we listen. What beautiful humility to see the holiness in the dark and to praise through singing. To find love and redemption in this broken world—we say Hallelujah. Even in the midst of death we praise life, in the midst of hate we see love, for the power of love is to redeem the brokenness; not to complete the work, yet neither are we to look away. Yes, Hineni, Here I am!

We can understand the path to awakening as a journey upriver, out of the mass of men and their lives of quiet desperation and into the heart of darkness where everything comes into perfect clarity, like a diamond bullet to the forehead. Like to guide on a sightseeing tour I'm sharing some points of interest, where bunnies danced where tigers lurk, where the waves break just right and where arrows rain from the sky, where you can catch a tan and where your once-human heart burns to a crisp. Ultimately, you may complete your mission and kill the Buddha, but only if the Buddha allows it, almost as if you were not sent but summoned. —Jed McKenna

Wisdom-maker, pacifist and poet Daniel Berrigan said: *One cannot level one's moral lance at every evil in the universe. There are just too many of them. But you can do something and the difference between doing something and doing nothing is everything.* Profound directive! Daniel Berrigan, prophet of peace, his commitment to being of service was sustainable through decades of the dark times of Aids and the Vietnam war working as a long-distance runner for love and justice. He lived in the presence of soul-making and the beloved, connected to his heart, with integrity, an authentic real mature human being. There is suffering in this world and still,

Suffering

Hineni Here I am. Arriving with a heart full of hope and dedication.

For there is always light, if only we're brave enough to see it. If only we're brave enough to be it. —Amanda Gorman

A universal experience, this invitation to sit with shattered hearts, the request is to be kind and gentle, compassionate to ourselves and others. Our internal communication, not to turn a knife on our tender heart, saying no when it's our truth, being grateful for the yes that opens doors. To bear loving witness. Impossible to remove suffering from this earthship we are all traveling on. Now to create presence and live with courage, openness, to transform our hardships and challenges into our teachings; from experiencing despair to eventually becoming ambassadors of love—turning towards life to experience it fully, as it appears.

Two hundred years ago Issa heard the morning birds singing sutras to this suffering world. I heard them too, this morning, which must mean since we will always have a suffering world, we must also always have a song.
—David Budbill

How to confront the Buddha's first noble truth, life is suffering. *Pain is inevitable. Suffering is optional* and still show up to live life fully. To meet life as it is, to become all of life, this is what it means to be fully alive. The world offers itself to us, and everything is in the manner that we see. How to direct our mind; essentially the Buddha is visible in all beings. All of existence is celebrating, become part of it—the sorrow and the delight—all a spiral, a rain of blessings. True wisdom arrives through our point of view, then all things are truly phenomenal. If you imagine that it's broken you certainly could imagine that you might fix it.

To be free of suffering. We must recognize that the suffering of one person or one nation is the suffering of humanity. That the happiness of one person or nation is the happiness of humanity. —the Dalai Lama

We turn away although the ground of life that carries loss interwoven with beauty and wonder is always here. Love sees life as precious and the grief that comes to us is proportionate and inescapable. A building that recently collapsed in Miami Beach was the site of great devastation and loss. As a small eleven-year-old girl sat on the curb with a book in hand the Mayor, Daniella Levine-Cava, walked over to see how she might be available to her. The child said *I am making prayers for my mother, she is somewhere in that rubble.* How to comprehend a world that is this too, for it is through and because of our love that we grieve. They go hand in hand. The more we open the more we feel, all of it, the mystery as well as the known, our heart fills and we see the beautiful innocence of a child as well as the longings and scarring. And each scar contains a lifetime's worth of lessons, teachings to understand.

Suffering

When you meet someone deep in grief slip off your needs and set them by the door. Enter barefoot this darkened chapel hollowed by loss hallowed by sorrow its gray stone walls and floor. You, congregation of one are here to listen not to sing. Kneel in the back pew. Make no sound, let the candles speak. —Patricia McKernon Runkle

As our heart joins the world and acknowledges suffering the wonder enters. Wonder as spiritual audacity, a fearless bravery of courage and confidence, of virtue and integrity—to imagine the holy vision as the miraculous. To train our mind to pay attention to the moment, not allowing the experience of unnecessary suffering overcome us: confusion, anger, separation, illusion, judgment; it's the true suffering of experiencing life as it is. And now to surrender, to build compassion, to not add to another's pain. Yes, inevitably there is sorrow and the possibility to meet ourselves where we are as well as to remember that each act tips the world one way or another. How to relieve suffering? How to see the world as it is? How to live in the smile—to smile to the sky, to the flowers, to the clouds and children, to the burdens and difficulties and allow the world to smile in return. To see the immense pain that effects others yet to be in the current of life and not succumb to tragedy, rather to live into the wonder and love as we continue and continue.

I watched His Holiness shift his mental state as quickly as stepping through an open doorway. The Dalai Lama's

♪ *Notes from the Ocean*

nimbleness of mind and heart is a good example of how the taste of suffering induces empathy followed by compassion in someone who has trained the mind and heart to use suffering as a medicine to open to greater love and care. His holiness is a powerful example for all of us today, as we face our imperiled world. His great and tender heart and his boundless wisdom open him to the truth of suffering and freedom from suffering. —Roshi Joan Halifax

To join the world, open and alert, to bear the sorrow knowing that many remain oblivious, how to come into a place of compassion, of benevolence? There are random tribulations like in the Book of Job, not the consequences of personal actions, inexplicable acts that point out our insignificance in the overall magnificence of life. Why me? No answer. Yes, there are human actions that directly create pain and suffering. Look deeply and you will see that in every turn of history there is a villain as well as a hero. Buddha had Mara. The bible has Haman and Mordecai/Esther. History and this present time continues to reveal the tragedies of the heart. Everything starts from looking more deeply into our own heart. This is how we carry the pain and suffering of our world.

We vent great passions by breaking into song, as we observe in the most grief-stricken and the most joyful.
—Giambattista Vico

Birth and death—when we miss the mark, when our integrity is compromised and our heart becomes restricted, how to discover our life raft, the one that lifts us from a dank small mud hole? Can we redeem the world through redemptive suffering? How to stand in the presence of difficult circumstances and maintain lightness in adversity? Yes, I am not alone. There is companionship and accompaniment. God's response to Job is *Hineni*. Here I am. Life is this and here I am.

When you eventually see through the veils to how things really are, you will keep saying again and again, This is certainly not like we thought it was. —Rumi

We may have a companion—a wife or husband, a child, a beautiful animal, a friend, and we turn to life, at first eager for this relationship and still this is not how we imagined. We see through the veils. Joyful for the other and in a sorrow that doesn't change the circumstances of what arrives. My darling I love you and cherish that you will walk with me in sorrow as well as dance with me in my joyful blessings. How to ennoble our suffering? We climb up and down the mountain, we see larger than the suffering, this is a transformative opening to true compassion. For ourselves, others and this planet. A deep understanding, the suffering of all sentient beings; not a boulder that we are chained to— it's a path of connecting to everyone on this earthship. Said Yeats: *We are put on earth in a little space, that we may learn to bear the beams of love. Love is like the lion's tooth.* The paradox, uncertainty of living, like sweet sorrow once understood we touch freedom.

How shall the heart be reconciled to its feast of losses? In a rising wind the manic dust of my friends, those who fell along the way, bitterly stings my face, yet I turn, exulting somewhat, with my will intact to go wherever I need to go and every stone on the road precious to me.
—Stanley Kunitz

And so we sing, solo, sometimes as a duet, at times with a chorus. We enter the fire, who is immanently present in the midst of the fire? Who accompanies us, sharing in the experience? *When things get really bad, just raise your glass and stamp your feet and do a little jig. That's about all you can do.* —Leonard Cohen. The world is on fire. Do we hear the divine weeping? We are here to love and be loved. We turn towards life. We dream, hope, suffer; the heart turns to hope in sorrow. To share the burdens of life, we sing and dance as tears roll to bear the impossible sorrow, we dream.

To dream the impossible dream To fight the unbearable foe To bear with unbearable sorrow To run where the brave dare not go To right the un-righteable wrong To love pure and chaste from afar To try when your arms are too weary To reach the unreachable star This is my quest, To follow that star No matter how hopeless, No matter how far. To fight for the right Without question or pause, To be willing to march into hell for a heavenly cause. And I know if I'll only be true To this glorious quest That my heart will lie peaceful and calm When I'm laid to my rest. And the world will be better for this And one man, sore and covered with

scars Still strove with his last ounce of courage To fight the unbeatable foe To reach the unreachable star.
—Leigh Mitch, Darion Joseph

It is not suffering we look for, it is the transformation of suffering. Used well—being present, rising above—not as an obstacle rather as reminders of our desire to awaken. Through suffering our compassion arises in her full flowering. —Dr. Paula Bromberg

May all beings be free from suffering
May all beings know peace
May all beings be loved
May all beings be free
May all beings know joy

Practice

Practice is what enables us to Live a life that makes some sense and is harmonious. It promotes the welfare of ourselves and other people. Practice is about what goes on with you in your life and how you feel as you live that life. What is important to you, what you struggle with, will change over time. But practice requires a continual return to exploring. Our sense of solidity gets stronger and stronger the longer we practice. Practice is what you're about.
—Charlotte Joko Beck

Everything, each moment carries the opportunity to practice. And practice brings us to the possibility of being here/now; cultivating awareness we open to life as it is happening. The work is to create a witness, someone who is home watching, observing the play, this leela, our dance of life, as it comes and goes. Not to fall into the narrative, to see with awareness, appreciation and gratitude towards all events: they are the food and fertilizer for our fate and destiny, for our planet dance that has brought us this far into the privilege of embodiment, aliveness.

Certainly circumstances come and go; are we fascinated by the play, do we fall into the story or will we use it for our own liberation? As we pay attention, mindful we begin to see the connections, to see life as it is. Our relatedness to impermanence, to continuation, to the intimacy of this beautifully orchestrated dance uplifts the sorrows in this temporal world.

Forget about looking That's how you keep your distance To see you have to step into the jaws of experience, chew and be chewed, until nothing is left. —Ken McCloud

Our practice strengthens the ability to allow our thoughts to come and go. What is the practice of practice—to know the difference between our thoughts and how things are. Discrimination is essential otherwise we think the waves, the swells, the current are the ocean, just as we imagine our thoughts to be real.

A practice: *Notice the part of you that is thinking about what you are thinking about. Then notice the part of you that is noticing. Keep doing that.*

And we can postulate further with the question: what limits our mind and our life? Filling the mind with thoughts we become what we think. Neuroscience research detected that an adult will process 70,000 automatic thoughts a day 3,000 thoughts per hour 7 thoughts per minute, traveling faster than light in speed. The mind is always moving. We go for a walk, the body moves, yet something in us remains unmoved. Lao Tzu stated that *stillness is the ruler of movement.* Consciousness is liquid like water: flowing. The mind is solid, rocklike, similar to ice as it freezes. Deeper is our core and being: witnessing self-awareness, watchfulness. How to allow for the spaciousness that is consciousness to arise? And so we practice, a wonderful place that becomes our refuge.

We come to practice because we don't have a sense of a deep and trustworthy place inside from which to live our lives. The slightest thing can make us wobble. So we think that wobbling is how to live. Our practice can help us discover a dependable source that's always with us—our imperturbable mind. Zen practice is about living ordinary life with our feet on the ground. We are an energy field interacting with multiple other energy fields, and how we interact internally and externally determines the shape and possibilities of our world. —Katherine Thanas

Your life is your song: sing it! This ongoing concert wisely orchestrated for the attentive listener, singing, what do we hear? What is the song of the raindrop, the waves, the cloud, the stars, this heartbeat, melodious birds; every element sings. The Kabbalists teach that each creature—even a blade of grass—has its own angel in heaven, and when we recite the world's songs each angel is empowered to sing in harmony. The beings themselves are sustained in the merit of these songs.

A bird gets up every morning and sings its song. It does not wait to hear what other birds are singing, nor does it look to see if another bird is getting more notice. It knows its song innately and sings, this is nature: knowing your song.
—Michele Oka Done

We choose activities to occupy our time and attention and we use those moments or are used by them. The external events are here as practice, a preparation to build a higher level of being or they become activities to distract us. Deliberate, consistent, commitment—to be alive is holy. Let's practice aliveness! External circumstances engage, entertain, catch us into argument, discussions, opinions; as if they are the real. Rather to use circumstances, external happenings as food and fertilizer for presence. Neither Covid, feminism, AIDS, or political parties are here to control our inner journey. The facts of our life appear as we cultivate compassion, they supply us with energy, understanding, possibility so as to uplift and redirect this world towards a new direction. Certainly we stand for the interdependence and freedom/equality for all beings. What stands in the way of waking up in this lifetime? Our practice is here in our life to bring attention and awareness to the how of what we are doing. Our attitude and centeredness, the way we live, uncovering what stands in our way of recognizing the beauty and privilege of being alive.

There's deep beauty in not averting our gaze. No matter how hard it is, no matter how heartbreaking it can be, it is about presence, it is about bearing witness. I used to think bearing witness was a passive act. I don't believe that anymore. I think that when we are present—when we bear witness, when we do not divert our gaze—something is revealed—the very marrow of life. We change. A transformation occurs. Our consciousness shifts.
—Terry Tempest Williams

We practice silently knowing there is no banner of recognition, no financial or certificate acknowledging *I practiced*, not a trophy; there is a profound recognition to remember, to not be lost in the wash of why we came here. To not be distracted from our deepest intentions, sidetracked to walk down roads that lead us away from our aspiration and yearnings. The daily practice is to remain clear and on track. Clarity and focus, what truly matters? Commitment, integrity, not getting lost in other people's stories, paying attention to a life deeply lived. Our practice is our own true self.

The foundation of all spiritual practice is love.
— H.H. the 14th Dalai Lama

The illusion that any practice like yoga, chanting or playing bowls will awaken or mature us is self-deception; repetition, showing up, presence, reliability, responsibility, integrity, awareness—who is doing the practice is key. Am I present? This may appear tedious, ridiculous, endless and going nowhere; and where is there to go—inside! We begin to learn what's unknowable, about beginnings, that our answers and explanations are not sufficient and that we are here to practice, to wake up to who we are, to experience this moment; it's our experience and our ability and desire to uplift our life that is the true mark of knowing.

There is no greater miracle than being present. Everything begins and never ends from this. You can't be present at your destination if you're not present enroute. —R.E. Burton

We create a witness—someone home—and turn to live our inner work regardless to outer circumstances. And how do we learn inner work? Practice. Practice paying attention, practice showing up for ourself and for others, practice generosity, practice to maintain attention, practice being in our heart, practice openness, follow tender loving-kindness—and over time with diligence and commitment uplifting moments of joy will peek through. Seeing what is, allowing that to be: the ground of life—uncertainty, impermanence; and still we continue our practice. To purify obscurations we have created, these accumulations—our motivation, attention and attitude increase our mindfulness practice—essentially it's the focus and uplifting of our heart to its natural state of awareness.

The path of love is not one option among many; it is the only path there is, for it is embedded in our very nature as persons. Even when I am alone I am in relation: to sky, air, memory, language, thought—and therefore to others. The human being who exists without others is impossible.
—Norman Fischer

In music space is as meaningful as the notes. A cup emptied of its liquid, a birdcage with the door open and nothing inside, a sky emptied of clouds, the bird disappears, a moment in time. We are the rememberers. Love is the capacity to take care of ourselves as well as holding a loving compassionate space for others.

♪ *Notes from the Ocean*

You are the sky. Everything else is just the weather.
—Pema Chodron

There are many ways to practice. Not a right or wrong way. Practicing is an invitation, since most anything can become our practice. I have traveled with many teachers in various traditions and each teaching promoted the possibility of awakening to the truth of who I am—through Sufi practice, through the Gurdjieff school, chanting mantras, learning movements, the musicality of language, traveling with the Guru, meditation, sitting with the dying, whirling, washing floors, cleaning meditation halls, spraying rose water on chairs and walls, cooking for the community, studying Torah and scripture, surgery, a car accident, other's judgements; each step imbedded, uplifted, opening the heart towards living into the unknown.

One does not discover new lands without consenting to lose sight, for a very long time, of the shore. —Andre Gide

Our practice is a letting go of the concepts, the beliefs; to serve life, this most sacred of gifts, through our actions we practice, looking deeply to cultivate awareness. Seeing the sacred in all things is the ordinary practice. The circumstances of our daily life serve as a reminder, are the invitation. Practice is available to us in each moment. Everything in our daily life can be accessed as our practice. Forgiveness, sacrifice, regret, cooking, shopping, walking, laundry, surrender, conversing—all is food for mindful living. Being present to the things we do throughout the day: we are practicing. While we are walking, if we know we are walking, not distracted, when attentive we walk mindfully. The key is in the knowing. This is a journey of the present moment. Knowing comes through awareness and is a state of knowing.

Practice smiling because at the same time a bomb is being dropped a rose is opening. —Natalie Goldberg

Koans and Haiku are two of the wisdom teachings we have access to, both wonderful reflections for our practice, and the more we practice the greater becomes our capacity for love and understanding. Koans—how to define the undefinable?

The koan is a paradigm of life itself. —Thomas Merton

Koans have been used for centuries to provoke, to free and train the mind from reason and logical sequencing and open inner space; our intuitive awakening. They are a means, a tool, a mirror to deepen and clarify, a spiritual practice to penetrate existence with intimacy. They are a training aimed towards self-inquiry. A basic question about the nature of reality, not a paradox, not a riddle, a stepping stone to go beyond words and ideas. Nothing to be solved or resolved; it's to sing and dissolve, to quiet the mind and our thinking, and here we are! Living into the, I don't know.

The koan is not a conundrum to be solved by a nimble wit. Nor, in my opinion, is it ever a paradoxical statement

except to those who view it from outside. When the koan is resolved it is realized to be a simple and clear statement of the consciousness which it has helped to awaken.
—Ruth Fuller Sasaki

This is the truth of what we select to read, how we eat, what artists we appreciate and the music we choose to listen to. We digest the consciousness of the person who wrote, painted, played music, cooked. With careful discrimination we pay attention to what is working at differing moments of our life. Impressions are the most important essential food for transformation. We live in a world of impressions. What are we thinking about ourselves inwardly and also towards others? Walking on the street and someone gives us a nasty look, or a smile—feel the difference in how that effects our state. What we are reading, listening to; to read Hafiz, Walt Whitman, to look at a Rembrandt, a Monet, to hear Bach, Gregorian chants, David Darling, Deva Premal; vibrations, tones to lift us.

Creating a harmonious home—we step across the threshold and behold—our spirit rises or falls. The light and colors chosen mindfully emanate a vibration to soothe the heart. How we receive the impression is based upon our openness and presence. Ordinary life assaults us with coarseness. At the same time we have higher possibilities to be something greater. True practice requires an inner vision, sensitivity to recognize that we are here to attentively serve. To be present in practical activities shifts us from automatic reactivity to thoughtful creativity.

Someone asked Nan-ch'uan 'How does one cultivate practice?' 'Nan-ch'uan replied,'It cannot be thought up. To tell people to cultivate in such and such a way, or to practice in such and such a way, is very difficult.' The questioner now asked, 'Then will you let students cultivate practice at all?' Nan-ch'uan answered, 'I cannot stop you.' 'How should I practice?' Nan-ch-uan said 'Do what you have to do; don't just follow behind others.' —Thomas Cleary

A popular koan is: *what is the sound of one hand clapping?* We go beyond the words, beyond meaning, beyond information, to the very question itself, to begin to deepen the question: what is sound? now we see we are without an answer or solution. How to live in this world of suffering and great joy and to hold both together? We drop into a quiet place without distractions placing our attention into this present moment. We meet ourselves most poignantly in moments of contraction and expansion. Are we present or swept away? Remaining open to the question possibilities emerge, self-awareness: moments of consciousness light the way. Seeing the circumstances the randomness of how we are pulled into choiceless attention and wanderings opens our vision to a higher reality. In stillness we are called to witness presence, the quintessential human task.

The Koan is actually in ourselves. Each one of us brings it with him into the world and tries to decipher it before

passing away. What the Zen master does is no more than point it out to us, so we may see it more plainly than before.
—Daisetu Teitaro Suzuki

Koans are often used as a method to disrupt the intellectual curiosity of a mind that struggles for an answer. We begin in childhood with large unanswerable questions. Why did my goldfish die and where did he go? How many stars are in the sky? How far do I walk to reach the moon? What makes tomorrow today? Where does the sun go at night?

And we continue to ask, questions that we carry throughout our lifetime: Why do children die? Who am I ? What am I? A practitioner wrote that *with the help of the koan we can show the deaf man the moon by pointing at it, and let the blind man know where the gate is by knocking on it.*

Can we access multiple ways to use our mind including the concrete sequential thinking that is so comfortably popular in this culture? How to sit in the small personal pond and leap/soar across the ocean into the absolute? To transform the mind and open the heart, this sudden encounter, one stroke, no trace, action and silence; and *the dancer becomes one with the dance.* How to enter this realm of openness, to live in compassion and wonder, in a world of great suffering, opening to both. The mind, the mind; to see through it, to direct it—this is the freedom. The moments that our mind wanders—this too is our practice. To notice and to pull it back to this present moment. The koan offers space, a puzzle, a surgical tool that opens edges to bring us deeper—beyond knowing.

Haiku is a refuge when the world seems chaotic, when you are lost, frightened, tangled, and nothing is clear.
—Natalie Goldberg

Haiku, a practice focused on a brief moment in time, creates a sudden sense of wonder with minimal words. This respected tradition, for some who carry strong rules, for others negotiating form becomes the revolution. Haiku positions things for us to see and directly experience—a powerful moment. The space, emptiness; what is missing allows our presence and imagination to step forth in aliveness and show up in a *Hineni, here I am,* present moment. No distractions —we are not here to entertain you with unnecessary inessentials. This is real, your whole life clearing the way.

The only real measure of a haiku is upon hearing one, your mind experiences a small sensation of space, which is nothing less than God. —Allen Ginsburg

Discovering a practice that offers us a way to enter a still space of mindful openness, whether it be haiku, yoga, painting, cooking, writing, movement; finding a form for what's formless is needed. Paring down to the essential makes each word, each motion profoundly meaningful. A practice is a beautiful tool to ennoble and dedicate time to become real, for what else is there to do as we unveil the world, as we open and nourish our heart, as we encourage others to join the wake-up team.

Two Haikus:

The evening cool, knowing the bell is toiling our life away.
—Issa

Snowstorm at the Refuge strange joy to see the world disappear. —Joan Halifax

Focused on this moment in time, music, rhythmic songs are simple, sometimes bluesy, stirring the heart, mind and spirit. How to see new, fresh, unseen until now, our practices whether they are koan, walking, dance, haiku, drumming, sitting; we shake up this old tree scrape off the dinosaur scales and voila! our true self appears eager for spaciousness; the freshness in awareness that is our real life. We pay attention, open and observe, this very moment. We are this practice—no longer outside me—it is me; and I show up!

We practice to open, to carry us further. Practices are engineered to crack us open and polish our spiritual heart. To be connected to higher energy and circulate a life force energizes and uplifts our life. Yoga, tennis, swimming, chanting, golfing, writing, hitting a bowl, singing—kirtan and bhajans, dance, repeating the name of God, prayer, counting prayer beads, meditation, kindling the Shabbat candles, sacred texts; all useable as we dedicate, become intentional, knowing that this too is a practice. We harness timeless ancient systems geared to open and deepen, to transform and bring us closer more intimate with what is sacred. For everything is holy; each moment reveals sanctity, divinity.

Yes! Education is remembering. Remember yourself. The world's greatest guitarist, Andres Segovia, was born with thick hands and stubby fingers. How could he play so exquisitely? He was often asked. Inside me I have a teacher he answered. And the teacher says, Andreas practice and the pupil in me says, Yes, I continue, I remember, I practice!
—Lillian Firestone

Ocean

Go to the ocean: there might be many waves, on the surface. The ocean exists without the waves, the waves cannot exist without the ocean. That's why we keep ourselves apart, not willing to lose our small boundaries and to become oceanic, becoming ocean itself. Becoming part of the vastness—to disappear into the ocean. —Osho

Waves come and go, they appear with the wind, just as suffering appears through the actions of life, so is ocean—vast, transcendental to time, pure reflection. The wave disappears to become ocean and yet does it disappear? The ocean reflects the sky, always changing, surrendered to the moon and tides and seasons, is life itself, this water filled with movement and vitality. Formless, yet taking on all forms, she is the source of all life on this planet.

The ocean is the personification of life's greatest trepidation: the unknown, vast and uncontrollable. Life originated in the oceans, possibly all that is arose from water. In *Siddhartha,* by Herman Hesse, Siddhartha studies with a ferryman who tells him that when you sit by a river, by an ocean, long enough, everything returns. Siddhartha watches the crystal movement of the water and learns that one of the secrets of the river/ocean is the water's constancy—it is always running but never runs out. *Have you also learned that secret from the river; that there is no such thing as time?* The ferryman tells him of the transcendental timelessness of the river/ocean, which brings Siddhartha to the realization that life is a river/ocean and that past, present and future are all one. The river is everywhere at the same time, at the source, at the mouth, at the waterfall, at the ferry, at the current, in the ocean, in the mountains, ubiquitous/simultaneously, and that the present only exists for it, not the shadow. The waters have many voices—*the voices of kings, warriors, of women giving birth,* of fish and shells, seagrass and pelicans, turtles and frolicking children—essentially all the voices in creation.

Enlightenment is when a wave realizes that it is the ocean.
—Thich Nhat Hanh

Childhood, adulthood, and old age are separated only by shadows, not by reality. Vasudeva, the wise awakened ferryman teaches Siddhartha how to listen to the water's wisdom explaining that even though he has heard the ten thousand voices of the river/ocean and its laugh he will hear yet something more from it. Siddhartha then sees many pictures and hears a voice of sorrow in the river. Through the river's teachings, Siddhartha comes to know that *time exists as an illusion that distracts us from life itself.* Time means mind—when the procession of thoughts creates time; when the clock of your mind stops there is no longer the thoughts of past and future there is only the present moment. Time is breath and we are reborn in each breath. All time is present at once. Siddhartha then understands that nothing separates the boy in him from the man, just as nothing separates his life as a samana, a traveling ascetic from that of a merchant; just as nothing separates me Paula from my life as a Psychologist from that of a writer from that as a beachgoer. Who we are at twenty in our essence remains to be who we still are at fifty. They all flow into one beautiful unity.

How do we learn to listen to the teaching of the ocean? The ocean represents eternity and the unity of everything in this universe. Siddhartha ultimately explains that love is the essential quality to have in the world, to love a person, a place, and the world; everything to be embraced for what it is.

The ocean can exist without the waves, holding on and letting go. Existence is like the ocean, we jump in and loosen boundaries to become oceanic. Yes! Observing tides and currents, moving away from the shoreline of our comfortable theories and opinions we know that waters run deep and are expressed through waves that are always on the surface. Remember the ocean and forget the waves, waves do not really exist without the ocean.

The sea, once it casts its spell, holds one in its net of wonder forever. —Jacques Cousteau

I remember living in New Mexico, land locked, ocean further than a days drive. Scanning the desert sand where sky/ocean meet in her spaciousness fed my heart. And weekly trips to the hot springs where warm bubbling water perpetually flowing was uplifting and energizing. We use what's before us, present to the *what is*, obliterating the *if only* along with random other criticism/complaints. A new partnership, seeing what is the mind settles bargaining voices to loosen, to drop away and become present to what's in front of us.

My metaphor appears as Ocean and I have also found this expansiveness in the desert of New Mexico, in the open Israeli skyline, in the upward vision called sky, in the heart of my beloved. Water is movement, flow, earth's water is always in movement on, above, and below the surface of the Earth. This is not only Planet Earth—it's also Planet Ocean. Every drop of water has life in it. And we depend on our oceans, makes the earth habitable as it manages climate—we feel the earth breathe as we stand before the sea. Waves, currents and cycling tides; scientists claim the ocean as the source of all life on this planet as well as being the embodiment for worry and concern in her unknown and uncontrollable temperament.

I remember living in Waipio Valley, its name meaning *curving water*, on the northeast coast of Hawaii, known as the valley of the Kings. This beautiful land has been essentially uninhabited since 1946 when a tsunami devastated the valley. Today you see taro fields, lush tropical vegetation, walking paths, orange and lime trees, sweeping sea vistas, dramatic tropical beauty.

♪ *Notes from the Ocean*

Between 4,000 to 10,000 people lived there when the great waves rolled through the valley. The sacred Waipio Valley an important site of Native Hawaiians, now less than 100 residents live amongst the waterfalls, taro fields and rivers permeating the valley. The hazardous conditions of the roads in imminent threat of slope and roadway closure is of such magnitude that currently all visitors have no access and all vehicles are prohibited.

At the coastline when the sea floor rises to meet the shore the incoming wave with nowhere to go but up surges to reveal its fifty foot height, and everything is carried away. Tsunami, a Japanese word that translates to *harbour wave* are a series of waves following seismic events. Unusual sea-level fluctuations create a wall of water, mostly generated by earthquakes under the ocean that displace the seafloor. This transfer of energy from the seafloor to the ocean, this force in nature continues to represent vastness and overwhelming impermanence. How to take care and generate energy towards ourself and others; our task is to protect and see what is not seen.

See and realize that this world is not permanent. Neither late nor early flowers will remain. Oh that my monk's robes were wide enough to gather up all the people in this floating world. —Ryokan

Approximately 71 percent of Earth's surface is water covered and the oceans hold about 97 percent of all Earth's water. Water also exists in the air as water vapor, in rivers and lakes, in icecaps and glaciers, in the ground as soil moisture, in aquifers. The power of the ocean waves influenced by the flow of wind on the surface of the ocean as currents are influenced by the heat from the sun on the equator and cooler poles. Tides caused by gravitational forces from the moon and sun, all three contain some form of movement—potential energy and slight changes can lead to much larger downstream effects that affect us as we go to our beloved beaches. The ocean itself is not responsible for the generation of waves, tides and currents, nor is she our adversary.

You have been walking the ocean's edge, holding up your robes to keep them dry. You must dive naked under and deeper under, a thousand times deeper. Love flows down. The ground submits to the sky and suffers what comes. Tell me, is the earth worse for giving in like that? Do not put blankets over the drum. Open completely. —Rumi

When our ocean is warm and the conditions right I go into the sea frequently. Peaceful, harmonious, a meditation and sanctuary, my heart song. Finding our place—it might be by a window that looks out to a tree, a local park, cafe, a particular spot. In South Florida it's my large multi-colored granite desk looking west over the intercoastal water, gazing out to the east I see the ocean, I write, have conversations with clients in my home sanctuary. There is a cushion to sit on, a rocking chair by a hand-built wooden bookcase, aromatic incense, ancient Tibetan singing bowls and bells, a place to feel nurtured and safe; my water heaven/haven.

The disintegration of this body does not touch me, just as when the petals of the plum blossom fall it does not mean the end of the plum tree. I see that I am like a wave on the surface of the ocean. I see myself in all the other waves, and I see all the other waves in me. The manifestation or the disappearance of the wave does not lessen the presence of the ocean. My Dharma body and spiritual life are not subject to birth and death. —Thich Nhat Hahn

I remember the moment when Thich Nhat Hanh left his body. I was sitting at the ocean on Hollywood beach and I read the notice on my cell phone. Looking at the sea Thay was there in the waves, smiling, waving *Hello dear Joyful Awakening,* reminding me, speaking directly to the heart of this person who has embraced Thay through my given sangha name *Joyful Awakening.* Everything is held in Mother Ocean. Always alive, filled with life, our initiation, a touch into eternity. Recognizing the inter-connectedness of all life, we take refuge in what becomes our sanctuary, breathing in vastness, expansiveness, our truest bodhisattva.

How to recognize the ordinary and uplift it to sacredness, the refuge that is our resource in daily life. And as this changes it's up to us to stay current on our walk throughout this lifetime. To notice what is our inner landscape and how that reflects light. Stepping aside to engage with this world as it is: this is our heart song. Swimming in the dance of this lifetime we rise.

Birth and death are the great passageways of life. The current of our soul's karma moves like the tide going out—to the divine sea of consciousness where all life begins. Home for me is liquid. The water wraps around my body the way the ocean wraps around the world. I love its texture, its light, its undulating caress. Years ago I had a prophetic vision. I saw a beautiful being rising out of a crystalline sea. I have carried this vision imprinted in my cells and often return to bathe myself in its all encompassing love. The evolution of our species; I have an unequivocal knowing that the earth's oceans will play a crucial role in our future.
—Chris Griscom

♪ *Notes from the Ocean*

The Children

Your children are not your children, They are the sons and daughters of Life's longing for itself. They come through you but not from you, and though they are with you yet they belong not to you. You may give them your love but not your thoughts, For they have their own thoughts. You are the bows from which your children as living arrows are sent forth. Let your bending in the archer's hand be for gladness; For even as the arrow that flies is loved, so loved is the bow that is stable. —Kahlil Gibran

My life work was directed by a chance encounter with a child, Noah, a 10-year-old in a head start program in East Harlem where I was teaching who had not spoken for seven years. I loved his casualness and innocence, his decisiveness to protect his inner world from intrusive outside opinions and definitions. He played and we twirled, using blocks to build intricate architecture and paint beautiful universes. We built and colored together silently, happily engaged we co-created worlds as he allowed me to enter his creative inner domain of enriched silence.

We often imagine that words are the only possibility of communication and yet sound existed before word. The source of creation audible and distinct was sound. Sounds enter, penetrate our bodies, there are moments when we hear the vibrations the electrical currents; all affect our neurological system. It is with this understanding that I make contact with the children, they are particularly open and touched by the psychic energy-life-current that reverberates within and around them.

It's so rich to enter into worlds of gardening, drawing, drumming, painting, smiling, climbing, walking together without chatter—it's the connection, the quality of the relationship that creates the intimacy. With presence we build a beautiful world, with practice we open into the heart of this world. Each of us has a wound, a scar, a story we live.

What is the source of our first suffering? It lies in the fact that we hesitated to speak. It was born in the moment when we accumulated silent things within us.
—Gaston Blanchard

Recognizing that the mind leans towards a dualistic perspective we have limited our ways of being on this earth. Fear, insecurity and the not-enough syndrome, the complaints and compromising smallness, ie.this is a great place although there might be a better one, this is a delicious restaurant but if I could afford it I'd like a different one, I would leave this job yet I don't want to lose the medical coverage—these habituated thoughts fill our mind with comparative thinking, worry, limitations; this way of living interferes with our ability to be satisfied and present. Our natural mind, the nature of mind, has no concepts or limits. Ordinary mind experiences life directly.

What will our children do in the morning? Will they wake with their hearts wanting to play, the way wings should? Will they have dreamed the needed flights and gathered the strength from the planets that all men and women need to balance the wonderful charms of the earth so that her power and beauty does not make us forget our own? I know all about the ways of the heart—how it wants to be alive. Love so needs to love that it will endure almost anything, even abuse, just to flicker for a moment. But the sky's mouth is kind, its song will never hurt you, for I sing those words. What will our children do in the morning if they do not see us fly? —Rumi

The Buddha compared natural mind to a gold nugget that is covered with dirt and grime. Cleaning the nugget we see the radiant shining gold, they are both of the same value. We see our thought forms: *I am no good, I can't do that, my feet are ugly, people don't like me, I am too challenging.* These are the obscurations that stand in our way of revealing natural openness, our spacious uncluttered clear mind. This discordant dissatisfaction, disharmony, opposes the individual and universal harmony of life.

We look not at the things which are seen, but at the things which are not seen; for the things which are seen are temporal; but the things which are not seen are eternal. —St. Paul

A child sees without comparing, analyzing, assessing, judging. A fresh new look with each moment. A zoo,

The Children

book store, walking trail, beach, ice cream, museum, parks, playground, not as thoughts to fill the mind and obscure the experience ie. like *when was this park built, how much does that painting cost, is there a better park in the next town?* This is the open innocent enthusiastic delight, the peaceful unfettered inquisitive world of child wonder. How do we keep this curiosity, uniqueness and interest alive throughout our lifetime? To age without dipping into lethargy and boredom and disinterest—to maintain the simplicity and fun of each moment. How can we guide our children to trust in the invisible and unknown, to encourage, support their creative imagination?

After leaving the sea, after millions of years of living inside of the sea we took the ocean with us. When a woman makes a baby, she gives it water inside her body to grow in. That water inside her body is almost exactly the same as the water of the sea. It is salty by just the same amount. She makes a little ocean in her body. And not only this. Our blood and our sweating they are both salty almost exactly like the water from the sea is salty. We carry oceans inside of us, in our blood and our sweat. And we are crying the oceans in our tears. —Gregory David Roberts

Noah lived in that simplistic world. Experiencing my non-intrusiveness he proceeded to speak to me. A word, a sentence, we laughed, pointed, twirled and danced. The school administrator, recognizing my ability, seeing that Noah opened through my presence offered me a job at Bellevue Psychiatric Hospital in the unit for children who were under observation for criminal behavior. There, in that institutional setting, I met and loved Mateo a five year old boy who had thrown his sister out of a window to stop her crying. His mother had been upset and not able to stop the baby's wails so Mateo was on one hand trying to be helpful, and apparently reactive and impulsive he created this terrible painful situation. No age appropriate idea of consequences his alliance with his mothers inability to stop her daughters outbursts or maintain a safe environment for her son with screens or rails on the windows, Mateo was now under psychiatric observation labeled a murderer. I found my niche, my life's work—to touch hearts of precious beings, to relieve suffering.

Emma, a 6 year old was brought to the children's ward—her mother had put out cigarettes on her arms and legs. Once recovered she immediately cried out, demanded to return to the mother who had abused her. The dilemma of toxic relationships and trauma bonding, confusing abusive behavior allows the wounding to shape our broken heart. Most of this world has grown up with some imprint of trauma, psychic wounding that shapes our life perspective, that blocks free-flowing development as well as shaping the neurobiology of addiction in the brain. Subsequently we treat ourself, others and this planet from that stance, an unknowing perspective filled with sadness, stress, disconnection, pain, betrayal, loss, cruelty, anger and frustration.

The Children

There is no outside, there is no inside; once the heart has become the Ocean of life, it accommodates all things and all beings. —Pir Vilayat Inayat Khan

Thank you for everything. I have no complaint whatsoever.
—Zen Master Sono

Each of us has our limp with its story to tell. We might paint it, dance our narrative, one client photographed garbage; we re-store as we re-member. From survival to thriving. At the root of our lives is a question, a koan. Not to be answered or solved, they are there to inform, direct, are a consequence of being born. Our life is not a question to be answered; there is no right answer nor problem to be solved, not a puzzle to be done; we are the caterpillar willing to change our way of being until one day we gradually open up to become, to release a beautiful butterfly. Bringing our exploration of what it means to be human, this is our invitation, our statement and expression, our practice to live into the heart of the world.

Systems that break down have the potential to reorganize themselves at a higher more robust level of functionality when we learn from the breakdown, instead of being diminished or crushed. This refers to the benefit we can derive from the psychological changes from our struggle with challenging life circumstances. These experiences can foster extraordinary resilience; they can foster hope; they can also foster awe and joy, with the ability to thrive in the present rather than being overwhelmed in the past.

Transforming our suffering doesn't mean that we are going to be returned to the state that we experienced before. But we can discover that suffering and loss have given us a greater ability to live in the present, rather than to be constantly overwhelmed by the past. —Joan Halifax

This is the only place to practice—here in the midst of this beautiful and troublesome world. From that place we will seek out a source of love. This is where we begin—we start from where we are. The place where we are standing is holy. To be in a place where there are challenges, hard work, commotion and still be harmonious and balanced in our heart. To not wobble. This is the context for our day labor; life. Our history is not frozen in time, it is alive and constantly unfolding. Allow for the contradictions, for impermanence; as recognition appears and awareness increases our breath connects us to the universal breath. Then our wounding becomes the wound, the world's pain and we release our personal story into universal truth.

To bring up children in small families is to give them small minds. That is one of the greatest misfortunes in the world—that children are brought up by small families. They get very small minds. If the children are living only with you, then certainly they have only one type of life to understand. They will become addicted to you, and that will be their problem for the whole of their life. A child is born to you, but he does not belong to you. Always remember that he has come through you. He has chosen

The Children

you as a passage, but he has his own destiny. Every child is born with great energy, but we destroy it. We paralyze every child, we cripple every child, and the society, culture, education, religion continues. Children's interests are natural—they are interested in the flowers, the butterflies, the pebbles on the seashore, in dancing under the stars in the sun, in the wind, climbing, swimming; we say lose your joy, lose your laughter, be competitive, make money, be possessive, fight for things that are meaningless. —Osho

Children with their honest questions, inquisitive, engaged, little Buddhas in process of growing, eager and open, they are the possibilities of the future. To be in love with life. A deep bow to the children: our hope, perspective, humor and promise, the dream and work, the reminder of our aspirations and soul connection. Matured innocence, love in her purest, our divine encounters—beams of sunlight.

I am playing I feel like hugging the wind and kissing and singing with the air, pushing the air far away. I am very, very happy. —Emma, 6 years old

When children play they are in the moment, exploring, imagining, growing, vitally alive. How to protect and nurture this natural seed so it grows to bear the fruit of what was planted and have the strength and fortitude, integrity and character to bear the weight of this world? Children and animals play instinctively. The adult world imposes form and limits on the fun and freedom that imagines and creates secret worlds in the world. To keep this quality of being present and add responsibility and maturity is our conundrum. It's an essential question and might be a salvation for our physical and mental demise in our aging process. Relinquishing the joy of living, reducing the fun in life ages us poorly. Most people having lost the pleasures of inner play that we had as children now turn to external fun regardless to life's circumstances. Travel, going to stores and shopping, spending money, entertainment, movies and television replace the simplicity of child's play. How to reclaim the secret and surprising world of our child's play?

Time is a child playing, moving counters on a game board: the kingdom belongs to a child. —Heraclitus

Teach all the children. Show them daisies. Teach them the taste of sassafras and wintergreen. Give them peppermint to put in their pockets as they go to school. Give them the fields and the woods and the possibility of the world salvaged from the lords of profit. Stand them in the stream, head them upstream, rejoice as they learn to love this green space they live in, its sticks and leaves and then the silent, beautiful blossoms. When it's over I want to say: all my life I was a bride married to amazement. I was the bridegroom, taking the world into my arms. —Mary Oliver

The Brain, The Mind, Consciousness

Scientists haven't investigated consciousness very deeply. They tend to think of the mind in relation to the brain, and yet the mind is something other than that. The mind is not a product of the brain. It is its own entity. Today's mind is a continuation of yesterday's mind. The mind is something worth finding out more about. The nature of consciousness is said to be clarity and awareness and it is difficult to argue that this is a product of the brain. The brain is part of our body, and consciousness depends on the brain but is still separate from it. Consciousness and the body are two different things. In the modern world we have neglected to explore how to find peace of mind. Technology is supposed to serve human values; therefore, it needs to be guided by human values. Technology of all kinds should be of benefit to humanity, as well as contributing to the protection of ecology. —the Dalai Lama

The mind has no definite location, outline, design, or absolute conclusive unmistakable definition and yet we still know that the mind exists and is real. Studies and investigations over centuries of scientific research continue to see the mind as constantly evolving. The brain is an organ, the mind is not and the mind is considered to be a most significant facet of a sentient being's nature.

♪ *Notes from the Ocean*

If you use your mind to study reality, you won't understand either your mind or reality. If you study reality without using your mind, you'll understand both. —Bodidharma

The Tibetan word for mind is *sen, that which knows.* The brain is not the mind, the legs are not our walking, the eyes are not sight, the lips are not kissing, the ears are not hearing. The mind is energy, aliveness and translates experiences while generating energy. When asked does the wind move or does the grass move the Teacher replies: *Your mind moves.*

Structural changes in the brain, named neuroplasticity allow us to work and then to decide how to manage what is built into our mind. Like training a dog or horse we have the possibility to change what has been programmed to bring balance into our brain and our life. Our brain has the remarkable ability to reorganize create and modify new neural pathways, to re-wire itself. In this way we develop from infancy to adulthood.

The brain, like a symphony orchestra is made up of groups of players that work together to produce particular results, such as movements, thoughts, feelings, memories, and physical sensations. Although these results may appear fairly simple when you watch someone yawn, blink, sneeze or raise an arm, the sheer number of players involved in such simple actions, and the range of interactions among them, form an amazingly complex picture.
—Dr. Robert Livingston

The Brain, The Mind, Consciousness

My life is designed within a motif of orchestral notes. All reminders to listen and remember, to be mindful of comings and goings from a sense of love. How does our lovingkindness shape our actions in this world? Rather than a practice of worry or suffering or anxiety I regulate my days with the practice of walking, going to the beach, music, beautiful organic food, writing, uplifted conversations and paying attention. Mindfulness, or resting in the mind's natural clarity is a powerful tool a practice that allows thoughts to come and go until one day we experience clarity of mind. Our mind is like a lake—ducks swim, lily pads sit, pebbles thrown in, boats ride on the surface, and still the essence of the mind is clear and remains to be water. Don't look for the calm in your mind—look at your mind calmly.

The essence of Buddha's teaching is that the mind is the source of all experience, and by changing the direction of the mind, we can change the quality of everything we experience. —Yongey Mingyur Rinpoche

Our mind creates happiness as well as fear and disappointment. All is mind and most people have many minds, not integrated, unable to hold to an intention, pulling us in numerous directions. The mind has a rotation system, first I like someone, then I don't like the person and the mind doesn't quite remember why it's annoyed at what once was pleasure and enjoyment. This moment I want to lose weight and the next moment the mind says eat the cookie this time, forgetting the other minds decision. Mind is a flux, it is a continuum of many minds. To live in the mind is to live a disintegrated fragmentary life.

We are like a drunken person staggering toward our goal.
—Michel de Montaigne

Every cell in our body, each thought in our mind, all feelings we have, every action we choose to take vibrates at a certain frequency. Thought forms have energetic vibrations, very subtle electric waves. The strength of our thoughts carries us great distances—plant a beautiful garden to nourish the atmosphere. The mind is a magnet, cultivate it for suppleness and flexibility, as well as to elevate and uplift the world.

Great is Mind. Heaven's height is immeasurable, but Mind goes beyond heaven; the earth's depth is also unfathomable, but Mind reaches below the earth. The light of the sun and moon cannot be outdistanced, yet Mind passes beyond the light of the sun and moon. The macrocosm is limitless, yet Mind travels outside the macrocosm. How great is Space! How great the Primal Energy! Still Mind encompasses Space and generates the Primal Energy. Because of it heaven covers and earth upbears. Because of it the sun and moon move on, the four seasons come in succession, and all things are generated. Great indeed is Mind! —Myoan Eisai

Without the mind the body will continue to function, it digests food; the body has its own wisdom and knows how to breathe and take in oxygen and other nutrients from the atmosphere. This mind is a wonderful instrument when we know how to use it. A well-trained mind is directed and guided by sustained intention. How to do everything with mindfulness and awareness of the present moment, mindfulness helps us come back to ourselves and calm our mental formations; to bring our mind back to our body so that our whole being is present to the present moment.

Everything is energy and that is all there is to it. Match the frequency of the reality you want and you cannot help but get that reality. It can be no other way. This is not philosophy. This is physics. —Albert Einstein

When I lived at a Fourth Way School, *The Circle of Angels,* I understood the essential meaning and necessity of bringing this helter-skelter multi-tracked mind to focus, to a consistent reliable integration. A long journey that continued and continued, that continues and continues. Beyond this moment.

Creating a witness, an observer, someone home who will manage the movie, this might look to be an orchestra leader who knows the instruments—brain, mind, emotions, harmony and has a great love for the music. And all is music, from country to blues to opera, from rock to international, from chants to popular; all expressing beauty through different shades and tones. Everything comes and goes while the witness, the observer—once we build her—remains as anchor.

Your true nature is that of infinite spirit. The feeling of limitation is the work of the mind.
—Bhagavan Sri Ramana Maharshi

We do have the possibility of slowing down the activity of the mind, as well as speeding it up; connecting to higher mind outside ourselves we come into presence. Openness. Open to the great possibility of living the questions, of living into the *I don't know*, of embracing impermanence. Direct contact with life brings us to silence. How to see without thinking, how to listen with openness; to live in the moment brings us to knowing life as precious, we are that; a tender beautiful treasure to protect and love.

Just realizing the meaning of mind encompasses all understanding. —Jamgon Kongtrul

We certainly wouldn't let an unruly untrained dog run around in our home. Then why do we live with a poorly disciplined critter roaming about in our head creating havoc at its pleasure and convenience? How to train our thoughts from interrupting our inner peace? This is the importance of tools and strategies to maintain a harmonious inner garden. I often use music to hold my mind steady. And ideas, like there are no good or bad thoughts: only thoughts. I don't want to add suffering to this world. Aware of suffering I practice to create a more sustainable world for the benefit, the welfare of all. Find what holds you to the higher, discover when to feed the wolf to save the lamb. The mind is bedrock, a source to guide and develop. We all have thoughts that roam through our mind: we don't have to live at the mercy of the invasive words that appear randomly in our head, that sabotage our inner peace and stability. The universal harmony of consciousness is our guide to life. The dance and attraction of the sun and the moon, the cosmic display of the stars and the planets, moving rhythmically, the regularity and rotation of seasons, all a masterful symphony, all essential chords and notes when we listen and know our own significance our own personal sound—musical note—in the composition, orchestration, called life.

Suffering follows a negative thought as the wheels of a cart follow the oxen that draw it. —The Dhammapada

The mind obscures our ability to see things as they are. Resting our mind allows the commotion, the dirt and confusion to settle and then to live into a clean clear space regardless of circumstances. Learning to lovingly handle physical discomfort as well as clearing mental toxicity is paramount.

When mind is weak, the situation is a problem. When mind is balanced, the situation is a challenge. When mind is strong, situation becomes opportunity. —Sai Muthu

To work with mind is to understand that it is both relative and eternal. There is my mind and the mind. My mind is that which includes the cause of my suffering and brings me to experience happiness. Life actually is as it is, and our perception and desires are where we indulge our distortions. Small mind seizes on emotional baggage, beliefs and fears and holds a screen in front of the possibility of awakening. The process of waking up is in the realm of the emotional life more than in the arena of our spiritual life. We may find joy in this earthly life as we pursue happiness; beautiful peaceful harmony is found in the bliss of the spirit.

There is a dance only you can do, that exists only in you, here and now, always changing, always true. Are you willing to listen? If you are, it will deliver you unto the self you have always dreamed you could be. This is a promise.
—Gabrielle Roth

Our unnecessary suffering which consumes a great amount of energy is built into our mind and comes with confusion and artful self-trickery. Appearing to be real, habits and years of routines created and supported by our mind arrives from mental chicanery, movement, commotion and dramas that interrupt and take us away from the peace and calmness of a quiet unoccupied mind. Mind is mind and when we stir it, attaching to our thoughts, allowing circumstances and life challenges to agitate it, we suffer. How can we navigate and maintain a healthy steady clear mind?

We all agree that training the body through exercise and diet and relaxation is a good idea, but why don't we think of training our mind. Once we see how our mind works we see how our life works, too. That changes us. —S. Rinpoche

The Brain, The Mind, Consciousness

The brain is a complex organ, a mechanism sending and receiving chemical and electrical signals throughout the body. This physical instrument records so we have memories to use efficiently, which is why we don't want our nostalgic sentimental memories to flood the needed ones that tell us where we live, how to drive, directing our mind to function. How does the brain work with the many changing minds we each have that so often are in flux? The body continues without the mind directing it. This main organ of the human nervous system manages thought, memory, emotion, touch, vision, motor skills, breathing, temperature, hunger; every process that regulates our body. And still so much is unknown and a mystery particularly around consciousness and the perception of reality—our brain interprets, controls and coordinates to make sense of this world within and outside of us.

The brain—is wider than the sky—for—put them side by side—The one the other will contain with ease—and you beside. —Emily Dickinson

Often we think that the brain and the mind are interchangeable. They are interconnected yet different. Separate and inseparable. On one hand we are our mind which is energy, and we have the possibility to both choose and change what is built into our brain. The brain, like a tape-recording mechanism documents and stores memories. The mind and consciousness are two phases of the same phenomenon. Awareness is flowing, creating an observer, a witness, someone who is present and available—a bridge between you and the world—freedom from our illusion of separateness. Life originates here!

The harmony of life can be learned in the same way as the harmony of music. The ear should be trained to distinguish both tone and word, the meaning concealed within, and to know from the verbal meaning and the tone of the voice whether it is a true word or a false note; to distinguish between sarcasm and sincerity, between words spoken in jest, and those spoken in earnest; to understand the difference between true admiration and flattery; to distinguish modesty from humility, a smile from a sneer, and arrogance from pride, either directly or indirectly expressed. By so doing the ear becomes gradually trained in the same way as in music, and a person knows exactly whether his own tone and word, as well as those of another, are false or true. An untrained person confuses these. Like a student of music, we train our voice and ear in the harmony of life. The attainment of harmony in life; to the ear every word spoken is like a note that is true when harmonious and false when inharmonious.
—Hazrat Inayat Khan

The mind's ability to know itself is the ingredient that creates an observer—letting us know when our mind wanders and becomes distracted. The focus shifts from taming the mind to training the mind. Following and training the mind we learn to recognize and release fascination, negativity, self-centered and possessive thoughts, worry and dissatisfaction. Mindfulness is at the heart of all training, an essential key to awakening. To connect to that witnessing capacity, to remain alert, watchful, is to move with sharp consciousness. Our direct experience is the precision of this present moment. To see through the lens of a clear mind we are just here—reflecting whatever is—this is clarity, when there are no thoughts we become pure perception. Self-indulgence and fascination both impedes and confuses our trek towards consciousness and we are lost analyzing, in opinions and self-deception, in our personal subjectivity.

The world—because it's largely unconscious—will always seek to invalidate and suppress our consciousness.
—Dr. Gabor Mate

Not to let anything stand in our way towards awakening we saturate ourselves with what is. Awakening becomes self-evident once we know that we are asleep. The recognition brings us to stand on a rung, the ladder we stand on as we rise upward towards awakening. We are in a dynamic relationship with the earth and as we find our footing, as we stand up in ourself this is the moment-to-moment life that carries the understanding that the world is me; bearing this, I pay attention. Consciousness is not mind activity, not entertainment, ambition or doing activity. The conscious experience in our brain can not simply be reduced to neural activity alone. Our consciousness evolves when we diminish mental chatter. We go out into the world and gather ideas and objects and imagine them to be precious. Fool's gold. To awaken is day labor, a practice of commitment, sacrifice, humility and transformation.

Our life is shaped by our mind. The mind is everything, everything has mind in the lead, has mind in the forefront, is made by the mind. What we think, we become. Suffering follows negative thoughts. Joy follows pure thoughts, like a shadow that never leaves. There is nothing so disobedient as an undisciplined mind, and there is nothing so obedient as a disciplined mind. The mind, the mind, the mind—this is the beginning and end of it all. The quality of one's life depends on nothing but the mind. —the Buddha

Attention

The dream of my life is to lie down by a slow river and stare at the light in the trees—to learn something by being nothing a little while but the rich lens of attention. And this is the core of the secret: Attention is the beginning of devotion. —Mary Oliver

To anchor the force of attention requires practice. Our mechanical reactivity diminishes the possibility of presence. Devotion grows from paying attention. And this is a critical issue for this world. Careful attention, developed devotion opens gratitude and compassion. Let us deepen our ability to gaze, to look out into this amazing world that we are accountable for that has been offered to us to protect and caretake. As guardian and custodians of the planet we recall our parents and school teachers reminding, in fact insisting, that we pay attention. Whether we questioned or understood the process and requirement needed for that directive often it easily passed us by. It is to resist the numerous distractions that come into play—the thoughts that float through our mind, the physical discomforts that draw our attention—an itch, a sound, an idea or old conversation, the urge to look around a room and unsettle our grounding placing our attention outside ourselves—the wanderings of our mind, all the relinquishments needed for us to create inner discipline.

To harness our monkey mind and train meandering thoughts is like training a puppy who doesn't maintain restraint; to quiet the automatized busyness through attention is an essential step. How are we able to love and cherish what we don't notice? The mind is our essential tool to develop enabling us to experience joy and commitment to a beautiful life.

Conscious attention is an instrument which vibrates like a crystal at its own frequency. It is free to receive the signals broadcast at each moment from a creative universe in communication with all creatures. In man, the smallest deformation of a balanced attention closes down this two-way communication. —William Segal

Buddha placed mindfulness at the heart of all teaching. So many on a spiritual path confuse their desire to still or drop the mind, falsely imagining that our focus is to stop thoughts. To look at our own mind amidst challenges—not holding attention during the difficult brings us to make mind a mysterious enemy. To study this instrument; to be at home as the driver, the one who knows and is behind the wheel called mind is where to place our attention.

The only demand from us is that our heart be purified by means of attention. —St. Simeon

Mindfulness, witnessing allows understanding to arise. This is about self-awareness and not the rigidity and tightness of forced discipline. To have the mind behave and control its wandering allows spaciousness; this inner spacial awareness is consciousness itself and there is no separation between the conscious awareness inside each one of us and the conscious awareness that's inside everyone else—having this recognition/experience will shift our way of being in the world. We are a cosmic spatial consciousness, connected and in all space everywhere. Whenever we reach inward with our attention we find this conscious infinite space and to focus—pay attention—we see that our deepest self is the same one self in all of us.

Love is attentive. And when people are attentive to you, you feel loved, because in love we pay attention to each other. It has been found that attention is one of the most important ingredients for any kind of growth, outer or inner. It's gardening, paying attention to yourself, and when we see the flowers of consciousness we have created the opportunity, supplying nourishment; within this communication of attentive care we flourish. —Osho

Attention is movement, it is not static. It's honed by athletes, it's visible when an animal is stalking prey. The intention and effort to develop attention strengthens our abilities. Begin with small aims, practice, bring our attention back to ourselves, then orient towards what is essential. Cows are preoccupied with the patch of grass that is before them: what is our gaze, our focus towards? Not to ignore what is here in front of us, being in the present moment, relinquishing meandering into the past and future, lifting sentimentality and melodrama to compassionate attentiveness: so much depends upon a green palm tree shading a motionless iguana who waits for the rain and for me to pass by.

Existence demands only one thing from us, that our heart be purified by means of attention. —St. Simeon

Everything to be sanctified, elevated, transformed into something most beautiful responds from attentive care. Life remodeled, now exalted and glorified. This happens through recognition and vision. Nothing is too small, even an ant has its source, is part of this holy dance, is miraculous, can be glorified—pay attention to a reminder of our interwoven fabric of life, each thread sustains us. Our attentiveness enlivens us. Becoming attentive to our inner needs is true gardening and when the flowers of consciousness bloom we are more available to see things as they are.

It has been found that attention is one of the most important ingredients for any kind of growth. Children, plants as well as our inner world; let's pay more attention to our own inner center. Shower your center with all your attention. —Osho

When asked to write down the highest wisdom Zen Master Ikkyu wrote down: *Attention, attention, attention. Attention means?* His student then asked *but what does attention mean?* Master Ikkyu then replied, *Attention means attention.*

To look deeper at silence, to offer our attention to the sound between the notes, the space between the words, the openness in our mind—is preparation to listen, to have aliveness, to cherish space and peacefulness. This is going to the heart of life; when we penetrate each moment with attention; taking away the distractions: this is beginner's mind, this is love.

Silence is something that comes from your heart, not from outside, silence doesn't mean not talking and not doing things; it means that you are not disturbed inside.
—Thich Nhat Hahn

That we can't touch the sky, the stars, the waterfall doesn't make them not exist. Our inattentiveness doesn't change reality—whether or not we see, things continue existing. The ocean does not disappear because a sightless person cannot see it or because a wave dashes the shore. We become impoverished from our undeveloped capacity to hold attention. Gratitude rests on our ability to see and experience the treasures, the blessings that appear in our life. Non-reactive attention to inner and outer experience requires a quality of active attention that curtails the automatic activity of inner dialogue and flow of images that distract requiring self-study and practice. To become a non-reactive witness to what arises, for it to pass through and for us not to create associations, not get stuck on the contents of consciousness—this is how we learn to surf the waves and glide over the currents of what arises. Our true nature is hidden underneath the changing images and noise of things that continuously happen to us.

You can talk about attention just like you talk about music. Human attention is at best a single note. A developed attention has chords, multi-tone whole-half, harmonics. Reality shifts happen all the time, and if you're working toward attention, presence and waking state, you'll need to get used to it and soon. —E.J. Gold

I am not my thoughts. Once we begin to see the difference between the contents of consciousness and consciousness we begin to free ourself from a bondage that opens the door to inner work. Our ordinary life, the continuity of daily practice and paying attention becomes the language of eternity. Our ancestors knew the placement of the stars in the sky without written records, the details of this universe were what they watched and where they paid attention. How to restore ourselves to the simplicity where attention is reality? Haiku and koan practice are two wonderful practices birthing purity of focus quieting the interfering noises that distract us from being present.

If you listen both to the sound of the bell and to the silence between the strokes, the whole of that listening is attention. Similarly, when someone is speaking, attention is the giving of your mind not only to the words but also to the silence between the words, If you experiment with this you will find that your mind can pay complete attention without distraction and without resistance. You can listen without any resistance because your mind has space and silence. Then the mind is a living thing, it is not dead.
—J. Krishnamurti

Attention is a full-body experience. Not only focused on the mind, it is an activity that engages a wholeness a stillness placing the mind in the heart. Attention is a transforming force—a bridge to carry theory and ideas into our practice and personal experiences. This treasured gift affords us the possibility to know ourself, to lift out of darkness, empower our life into light through developing inner attention. Breathing, we pay attention to the body; anchoring presence we become alive.

To pay attention. This is our endless and proper work.
—Mary Oliver

I traveled and lived with a Sufi teacher, Adnan Sarhan, director of the Sufi Foundation of the Shittari order, a master of non-intrusiveness who had a system of spiritual practices that are seated in breath, movement, chant, prayer, fasting, belly dance and drum. Movement is a training ground for sustained attention. Gurdjieff created sacred movements to access essence and become available to higher and finer universal forces. He said that we move the same way that we live; in this way learning sacred movements places us in a position to see the reality of who we are. They are a method to know ourself and be freed from the limit of mechanical habits and unconscious behaviors. The goal is not the movements in themselves, they are the means on the way—the goal is the person. The challenge of the process is not so much on the physical level. The movements are rather simple—what is demanding has to do with our quality of attention, with our presence—and that is what is being developed throughout the process. As we look for a state of attention without tension a moment arises that connects us to the whole—that affects us forever—an experience of the sacred within us. My years of practicing the movements brought me to tap into a greater reality through the development of a certain quality of attention and relaxation to realize that deep within myself there is a still point that is the ground of my being. This inner dance of attention. How to stop inner movement? There is a quality of energy behind our thoughts and feelings. This practice of movement and breath releases identification with sensory traits that are associated with daily life. Movements train us to keep our attention on the task at hand and our ability to direct our attention allows us to apply it to our inner work rather than get lost in fascination to the activities and images of daily circumstances. When our focus of attention is taken over by the events at hand we lose our ability to be present.

Live in the present before it passes you by and becomes the past. —Adnan Sarhan

Directing our attention so it is not only towards ourself places us into the community of humanity. Moving from a preoccupation with self we expand into a larger world, one that magnifies depth and the possibilities of life, to dis-identifiy with illusion, fascination and self-involvement; this continues our awakening process, our journey toward consciousness. Beautiful golden coins pouring from the heavens require our attention, our ability to see and be available to receive them. To be at the service of mindful attention we open to the calling that is the measure of who we are. We are our attention: where we place our mind, our heart—here we are!

A tool for transformation—attention—and the quality of attention which maintains its direction—since ordinary attention is not sufficient—supplies and directs energy. Mindful attention creates the connection needed for awareness, creativity, deepening maturity, responsibility and life purpose.

The point is to perform every activity, from playing basketball to taking out the garbage, with precise attention, moment by moment. —Phil Jackson

An Apache trained acquaintance of mine used to throw his head back, laugh into the sky and say 'what will you buy with your attention today?' —Scout Cloud Lee

Spiritual Friendship

Stay together, friends. Don't scatter and sleep. Our friendship is made of being awake. —Rumi

Open to the call of the other; listening, paying attention, seeing ourselves as we are we step into an honest dignified life, a life of kindness. Knowing our connectedness to each other and to the world, our openness as we walk this path of love sustains the journey. Practices remind us when we are closing down. To practice openness to the differences in people—in the mirroring reflections we receive valuable information. We are a looking glass, a reflection for self-inquiry, to observe, watch patiently for everything to unfold as it is.

Friendship depends on trust, not money, not power, not mere education or knowledge. Only if there is trust will there be friendship. Trust is related to whether we have a sincere motivation. If we are sincere in taking care of others, if we protect their lives and respect their rights, we'll be able to conduct our lives transparently and that is the basis of trust, which in turn is the basis of friendship.
—His Holiness the 14th Dalai Lama

Community/sangha, each moment opening to life. As we bear witness to the suffering and sacrifices in this world to show up in compassion, with courage, hope and love for ourselves and for each other, evokes this deepening—matured friendship. Our spiritual friendship rests upon integrity, our willingness to keep our questions alive. To be responsible for ourselves, a daily practice of accepting and embracing ourselves with tenderness. Our practices are our teachers.

Neighbor is not a geographic term. It is a moral concept.
— Joachim Prinz

I remember the year I asked myself, listened deeply to the question: what is a friend? Rumi, Kabir, Hafiz, amongst other poet mystics name friend as beloved. No separation: when I bow to you, you are bowing to me. This reverence of loving continues—friend, partner, companion, beloved.

Ramakrishna said that he met his Lord in all the people that came to him. One clue to spiritualizing our relationships is to realize that everyone is a different facet of the diamond of God. The way to begin to understand that is to enter more deeply into what the mystics call 'unity', which is knowing that everything in reality is reflecting everything else and is everything else. —Andrew Harvey

Mystics see the relationship with God through a lens of love, one of friendship. The intimate friend, comrade, partner, the beloved who mingles with me, as close as the beating of my own heart. Friendship is an enduring heart-to-heart companionship as we sail together through the seas of time, a place of refuge, a treasure; horizons expanded we touch.

One night I saw God Almighty in a dream. I said to God: 'It's been sixty years that I have spent in the hope of being your friend, of desiring you.' God Almighty answered me: 'You've been seeking me for sixty years? I've spent eternity to eternity befriending you.' —Sufi Hasan Kharaqani. On the entranceway to Hasan Kharaqani's shrine is inscribed a simple poem: *Feed whoever comes here. Do not ask them their faith they deserve a daily bread in my house, of course! Since they were worthy of a soul in God's court.*

The distinction between *I* and *you* disappears in true intimacy. Love is obscured when we close the door to our heart. Opened, love pours forth. The wave disappears and becomes the ocean; an introduction to the possibility of holding our nature while absorbing the reality of others we walk with in this community named humanity. There is no right or wrong—all is a reflection. To communicate with the heart we become human, this is a spiritual courtship. Being together, recognizing another ancient traveler on our journey to the still center we become mirrors for each other reflecting divinity.

The self is revealed only in relationship. —J. Krishnamurti

The entranceway is this relationship I have with myself. Everything begins and emerges within this friendship I create with self, until one day this self no longer needs outside affirmation. To befriend love is to befriend humanity. How to release and move away from the personal jabs when we imagine ourselves falling short of any inner criteria we secretly harbor. As if there is a right and wrong way, as if I'm not good enough. Where do these critical voices originate if not in family, school, our culture, somewhere outside ourselves. And now they persist. Our friend eases the sting, is here as a balm and reminder of lovingkindness, as well as holding us to our highest intention. These inner voices that claim and rob our peacefulness. How to relinquish the sounds, letting them pass through without indulgence or fascination, to create voices that tenderize the heart. For the heart is the nucleus of this entire existence in our quest for the imperishable, our striving to live in a conscious way. Within this education of the heart are always others. They are the stuff life is made up of, reminders that everyday life is the practice, a compass, a deepening of the spirit to serve the world and mend this broken creation.

And once the storm is over you won't remember how you made it through, how you managed to survive. You won't even be sure, in fact, whether the storm is really over. But one thing is certain. When you come out of the storm you won't be the same person who walked in. That's what this storm's all about. —Haruki Murakami

My book, *The Way of the Lover,* speaks to relationship as a spiritual practice and path. We live in relationship to everything: our home, the earth, ocean, computer, car, books, the truth, integrity, child, dog, understanding, marriage, the beloved, meditation, family, mind;

to all of life's deepest truth. Our relationship to all and everything is the elevating inspiring meaningful honesty we have. There is no me awakening; as long as there is suffering we all suffer. This is the practice. No division, no separation, no discrimination. We are here, we practice, we serve.

Let us choose one another as companions. Let us sit at one another's feet. Come a little closer now, so that we may see each other's faces. Inside we share so many secrets—Do not believe we are simply what these eyes can see. Now we are music together, sharing one cup and an armful of roses.
—Rumi

Yes, we have the great possibility of learning from each person and experience we come upon. Our great teacher is the mirror reflecting an aspect of ourself for us to deepen, to dislodge; we are all and everything helping us arrive to a place of compassion, for we contain multitudes, particles that all point the way as we embrace and carry the teaching forward. Ah, to know we have companions to walk along with, we are all positioned to guide and uplift tenderly, to ask of ourself and each other, how can I be more loving?

Your heart and my heart are very very old friends. —Hafiz

Teach, said Gurdjieff, *so you may learn.* This is true service and within the process and development of our friendship, our relationships, we discover that our true self is what we have always been looking for. And that unfoldment arrives through relating, through smiling at our lies, deceptions, illusions, finally we might stop the endless childishness, to become the few who arrive matured with emotional intelligence into real adulthood, the priceless treasure of awakening!

To love someone long-term is to attend a thousand funerals of the people they used to be. The people they're too exhausted to be any longer. The people they don't recognize inside themselves anymore. The people they grew out of, the people they never ended up growing into. We so badly want the people we love to get their spark back when it burns out; to become speedily found when they are lost. But it is not our job to hold anyone accountable to the people they used to be. It is our job to travel with them between each version and to honor what emerges along the way. Sometimes it will be an even more luminescent flame. Sometimes it will be a flicker that disappears and temporarily floods the room with a perfect and necessary darkness. —Heidi Priebe

Our friends on a spiritual path whether face to face, always heart to heart create a true family of choice. Our sanctuary and harbor, our point of contact with love. A reminder that friendship is a creation of love, connection and grounding. A bridge linked to ourselves. This consistency on the physical plane is a reminder that regardless this person is available both in our heart and sometimes via a text or phone call or physical touch to anchor us into the present moment.

♪ *Notes from the Ocean*

Sharing values and intentions, we choose connections that resonate with higher vision. This is the verifiable family, the community of the heart.

Without love, life is impossible. We have to learn the art of loving. This world very much needs love. I am more and more convinced that the next Buddha may not just be one person, but a community, a community of love. We need to support each other to build a community where love is something tangible. This may be the most important thing we can do for the survival of the Earth. We have everything except love. We have to renew our way of loving. We have to really learn to love. The well-being of the world depends on us on the way we live our daily lives, on the way we take care of the world, and on the way we love.
—Thich Nhat Hahn

Maturity

True maturity is being willing and able to show up for all of life's meetings. Maturity is knowing that the world is constantly creating you moment by moment, but also that you are creating the world as you come forward to meet it with your skills, talent, and activity. —Norman Fischer

Awakening is maturity. We ripen like a beautiful fruit, a vintage wine, a succulent ready to be picked and indulged. Adulthood does not appear equated with maturity, this inner integrity that resonates love; this being responsible, non-reactive, compassionate is a creative force. Mindful intentional innocence; blaming and complaining are eventually relinquished uplifted to responsibility; to stand behind our collection of moments, owning our experiences. Who is this being having lived in this way? Maturity re-claims our lost innocence and places consciousness behind it. We come to life-wisdom, our walk through life, owning and understanding our experiences, the voices we embody, using them wisely. Transforming oneself. Spiritual rebirth is our flowering into awakening with the awareness that *this world is a beautiful place to be born into, what a wonderful world* even with its absurdity, violence, contradiction, inequity, irony, and nonsense. And how to live holding paradox, now carrying enthusiastic encouragement as youth, vitality and innocence slip away to face the truth of life: impermanence: change, the essence of life is built into being human—our bodies contain the available wisdom that include the tribulations and sorrows of this world. All cellular information used to mend the torn fabric and evolve matured love. Forgiveness is an essential step on the rungs of the ladder of maturity, and when we miss a critical foothold we remain mired in our immature adolescent behavior.

As our mental and physical capacities diminish as we get older, it's like an old piece of cloth that begins to become a little worn, and in places threadbare. It just means that the light shines through it that much more easily. So, it is not in any way something to be lamented or regretted. On the contrary, As the density of the mind softens and becomes more transparent as we get older, maybe it loses a little bit of its articulation (but) that doesn't matter because the light of being just shines through it more easily.
—Rupert Spira

We walk this path carefully knowing that our resolution our peacemaking does not necessitate external understanding or cooperation. What freedom within the awareness that the resolution is made within ourself, it's in our own heart. Forgiving ourself for falling short of expectations, forgiving those who have died and left us bereft, being compassionate to our desire for kindness when we fall short; all ingredients necessary to create loving awareness.

The living river of your life is continuously changing. Drink from it. Let that taste tell you how to move. When those who love meet each other's eyes, an expansion comes that cannot be contained in what the pronouns refer to, you and I and we, those imaginary beings. —Coleman Barks

Consciousness/awakening is maturity. Awareness is communal, consciousness is a shoreless infinite ocean. Living life as celebration. Allowing grief, holding sorrow and joy because everything contains everything else, this principle of interpenetration; we respond to life as it is without getting lost or overtaken in a sea of despair, in an ocean of delight.

Hope is not a lottery ticket you can sit on the sofa and clutch, feeling lucky. It is an axe you break down doors with in an emergency. Hope should shove you out the door, because it will take everything you have to steer the future away from endless war, from the annihilation of the earth's treasures and the grinding down of the poor and marginal. To hope is to give yourself to the future—and that commitment to the future is what makes the present inhabitable. —Rebecca Solnit

Living with integrity, maturity is both path and way. The first rung as well as an upper step on the ladder. Our work is to wake up. This is maturity: being real— to awaken others through our compassionate presence. The most basic and fundamental step is integrity— taking responsibility—to stop blaming and stand at the center of our own life. A place to put our feet and hands as we climb upwards, our ascent. Support for ourself and for others. Aware that we create our suffering, not our parents, not the culture or society, not the economic or environmental conditions, not the political climate or the educational system. Maturity carries stability and reliability—we show up in awareness to the circumstances having the capacity to be authentic to situations as they arise. Playful, alive and present; yes, this is presence: attentive, appreciative and aware of the wonder and beauty of existence. Moving from woe to wonder we plant seeds of poetic magic.

What is true maturity anyway? There are answers to most of life's most important questions, but they are never final, they change as we change, Maybe true maturity is finding a way to keep such questions alive throughout our lifetime. For when there are no more questions, we stop maturing and begin merely to age. —Norman Fischer

There is no guideline for authenticity. Living open, being real, minimizing distractions we encounter the call to respond to the experience of others and to the incredible pain and suffering of the world. When we contact another are we open? Do we listen? Are we receptive, available? How do we touch and enter another's life? What do we do with this life? All of this is a practice on the continuum of maturing. How is it we are to use this lifetime and serve ourself and the world with the generosity of our lifetime of experiences digested and savored, our ongoing practices that have brought us to be present with life as it appears? How to cultivate maturity and align adulthood, aging and maturity? Awakening, learning to love, compassionate awareness of others, a life of service to understand the generosity of true deepened maturity. What responsibility to real-ize, to make real our knowing, to mature, witness, stand behind what matters and to then place ourselves in the heart of the world!

I believe that we are put here in human form to decipher the hieroglyphs of love and suffering. And, there is no degree of love or intensity of feeling that does not bring with it the possibility of a crippling hurt. But, it is a duty to take that risk and love without reserve or defense. —Allen Ginsburg

Reclaiming the purity and softness of our birthright, to hold steady and still in the presence of love, listening as the other empties her heart, relieving suffering. Our gift this possibility of easing the corruption and toxicity inherent in our systems—political, educational, social, cultural, which has exploited, conditioned, disenfranchised us from our heart: how to reclaim the wonder and freshness? Maturity is the flowering of consciousness, living into the present moment with awareness and presence. Yes, we reclaim the sacred, now wiser, open and hopeful.

We are merely living out a dream of maturity, a set of received notions and images that passes for adulthood. What does it really mean to grow up? How do we do the work that will nurture a truly mature heart from which can flow healing words and deeds? —Norman Fischer

♪ *Notes from the Ocean*

Death and Compassion

The moon and sun are eternal travelers. Even the years wander on. A lifetime adrift in a boat or in old age leading a tired horse into the years, every day is a journey, and the journey itself is home. —Basho

How have we been practicing, preparing for our death? This ongoing truth we encounter, the agreement we signed up for the moment we entered this life. And reality appears throughout life in disguises called loss, endings, dissatisfaction and resistance. As we age we step out of the familiar to enter a world outside our known home. We move forward into nursery school or kindergarten, leaving what we knew as we expand into the unknown, away from family to create a new community. We know that the difference between being alive or dead is a single breath; impermanence: mortality and inescapable death.

In Praise of Craziness of a Certain Kind
On cold evenings my grandmother, with ownership of half her mind—the other half having flown back to Bohemia—spread newspapers over the porch floor so, she said, the garden ants could crawl beneath, as under a blanket, and keep warm, and what shall I wish for, for myself, but, being so struck by the lightening of years, to be like her with what is left, that loving. —Mary Oliver

Jane Goodall, when asked what's next in her decades-long career did not hesitate: *Dying,* said Goodall,

Death and Compassion

eighty-eight years of age. The renowned primatologist and ethologist who first discovered that chimpanzees, like humans, use tools. *Ten years ago,* Goodall said she *would have said something like visit the remote areas in Papua, New Guinea.* Now Goodall said *she can't do that.* Having thought about death *there's either nothing, or there's something. If that's true, can you think of a greater adventure than finding out what it is?* Goodall has been a consummate question-asker. She speaks of the first questions she asked wondering *how worms move without any legs,* trying to figure out *what hole on a chicken was large enough to lay an egg* and *why Tarzan married the wrong Jane.* When millions make ethical decisions it makes a difference. *Nature is resilient. Everything is inter-connected. Act locally, think globally. And, yes,* said Goodall, *dying will be my next adventure.*

When we look at the ocean, we see that each wave has a beginning and an end. A wave has, can be compared with other waves, and we can call it more or less beautiful, higher or lower, longer lasting or less long lasting. But if we look more deeply, we see that a wave is made of water. While living the life of a wave, the wave also lives the life of water. It would be sad if the wave did not know that it is water. It would think, 'Some day I will have to die. This period of time is my life span, and when I arrive at the shore, I will return to non-being.' These notions will cause the wave fear and anguish. A wave can be recognized by signs—beginning or ending, high or low, beautiful or ugly. In the world of the wave, the world of relative truth, the

wave feels happy as she swells, and she feels sad as she falls. She may think, 'I am high!' or 'I am low!' And develop superiority or inferiority complexes, but in the world of the water there are no signs, and when the wave touches her true nature—which is water—all of her complexes will cease, and she will transcend birth and death.
—Thich Nhat Hahn

I remember at the spiritual community, a Fourth Way School, named *The Circle of Angels*, we were offered an exercise to bring something of value and put it on a table where another student could choose to have the item. Looking back I see this as a continuing preparation for our death, when we give up our life belongings—the special chair, jewelry, books, acquaintances, habits, the body; not things taken on our voyage away from this life.

What Gurdjieff literally hammered into me as a child was that death is inevitable; it is one's ultimate and only destination. The innate understanding of this fact—every minute, hour or day is something one could experience fully, I understand. To be aware of what I am doing when I go out in order not to be maimed or killed, reinforcing the state of awareness to get everything out of whatever you may be doing at the moment to not be unconscious or unaware when you do meet death. Through Gurdjieff I understand that, like an arrow, this is aimed at one target: death. Life may have myriad bypaths, diversions or dreams along the way, yet the final destination is the grave.
—Fritz Peters

Death and Compassion

We know when we see the children that we won't be here to participate in their old age, just as they were not here to participate in our childhood. We don't talk about these poignant remarkable truths of life. Children easily ask the questions: why is that person sad or crying or in a wheelchair or have one leg? Adults learn to close down, to say *shush that's not nice to ask*. We can learn to train the mind and heart to move towards the difficult and embrace the true ground of life, to live in the I don't know mind, to embrace the reality of impermanence, to enter the realm of compassion.

In the village graveyard a seven-year-old boy cries silently 'Why, why?' At his sister's burial. His eighteen-year-old sister who taught him poetry who knitted him a sweater whose soft black hair hung to her waist is going underground. Now she goes to terra incognito. The boy cries silently, 'Why, why?' As a provisional answer they build a small tombstone for her and lichen grows over very slowly. One lovely morning the boy becomes a tombstone and lichen grows over very slowly. Tomorrow you still hear the song of the lichen:'Why, why?' —Nanao Sakaki

There is a wonderful story about the possibility of reliving a section of our life again. P.D. Ouspensky in *The Strange Life of Ivan Osokin* describes how Ivan asked the magician for the opportunity to redo his past and what he considered to be his failures. Can we awaken or do we remain imprisoned in our forgetfulness and sleep? Given the possibility to live in awareness knowing the truth of life: impermanence and death, how do we live with the knowledge that this brief moment in time is miraculous, is precious? How to live into the now of our life? Self-observation creates a space, a ledge to stand outside and see the play as it unfolds without our judgments, opinions, and self-absorption. Knowing that the future will be can we act responsibly in the light of this knowledge?

Osokin comes to realize that to truly change he has to give his life over, sacrifice his life for awakening. Not able to change the narrative and knowing the outcome—most people choose to imagine that different choices might alter, change the story. Sacrifice the false self, the strategies and illusions that until now have brought lifetime rewards. The film Groundhog Day was based on the book *Strange Life of Ivan Osokin*—how to escape the spiral, our being trapped in a repeating loop, that to save our life is to endanger it.

Ivan visits a magician and, after relating the troubles of his life asks for the opportunity to live his life over, to reformat the inner hard drive now with the knowledge of what will happen so that he might make new choices going forward. The magician informs him that *you will remember everything as long as you do not wish to forget* and through mysterious miraculous means transports Osokin to the time when he was a young boy in school. Osokin almost immediately begins to make the same choices over and over again. This time he knows the outcome yet continues to repeat his behavior with the painful impending realization of the consequences. He can see his own choices and futilely struggles against the inevitability of recurrence.

Telling a story about human life and being caught in a cycle—a story about how to live—dropping into the present moment this day becomes the best day. Renewal, redemption: what is it to live knowing impermanence?

This very night, while you lie quietly in your bed, open your eyes. Now, look out your window! For even at this yawning hour, so many of your friends are working to keep this world magical! Yes, they are the ones who make new stars and put them up. The ones who will make sure that the sun gets down safely. Now, while you sleep tonight imagine what you most would like to do to help keep the world magical? For you know that one of these nights your friends are going to tap on your window and invite you to become one of the Caretakers of Wonder. —Cooper Edens

This moment a miracle, how to live within the understanding that this brief moment will be shortened, wiped away. The sands of time move quickly. Let us not turn away. I remember the egg timers we had in our home, the sand slowly moving into the next portion and when I was young such a slow eeking out, and now as I age somehow ironically the same sand moves swiftly. The vehicle, this body, this leaky old boat wearing out while the spirit, the soul expands, adds to the light and frequency, speeds up energetically. Yes, the greatest mystery of life is not life itself, it's death; our daily experience with impermanence—to be shaken out of the dream is to look for what really matters. Life and death cannot be separated they are aspects of each other.

If grief made a sound the whole world, the atmosphere, would be humming. —Stephen Levine

Such tender compassion we might hold towards ourselves, living in this fragile vulnerable container called a body while we move throughout our years gathering experiences. And to continue to live into the questions, to embrace the questions as doors that open into a larger field. Expansiveness, a deep bow to the mystery. Let us sing our redemption song our Hallelujahs as we dive into the heart of the mystery to make love/art with the unknowable unpredictable; finely tuned we rise saying Yes to life and death as one.

Pretend you are an old man/woman watching children play. Just watch, delighted, even though you know the obstacles, the heartbreaks, the sorrows, the jolts. You know these things. Now is your time to stand at the edge and watch the water flow by. Just watch, without getting caught in the current. —Yongey Mingyur Rinpoche

This is what I want in heaven…words to become notes and conversations to be symphonies. —Tina Turner

Death and Compassion

From time to time Reb Elimelech of Lizensk would say: *I will earn eternal life.* People asked *how he could be so sure: Is it not written be exceedingly humble, for the end of humankind is the worm.* Elimelech replied: *Never fear, I will earn it. When I arrive at the gates of Eden, they will ask me: Did you learn enough Torah? I will say: No. They will ask: Did you pray with enough fervor? I will say: No. They will ask: Well did you fulfill the other commandments as you should have? I will say: No. Finally they will ask: What of your good deeds? I will say: I had none. And then they will say: An honest man! Come in, come in.* —an inspired Hasidic teaching

*Do not say that I'll depart tomorrow
because even today I still arrive.*

*Look deeply; I arrive in every second
to be a bud on a spring branch,
to be a tiny bird, whose wings are still
   fragile, learning to sing in my new nest,
to be a caterpillar in the heart of a flower,
to be a jewel hiding itself in a stone.*

*I still arrive, in order to laugh and to cry, in
   order to fear and to hope,
the rhythm of my heart is the birth and
   death of all that are alive.*

—Thich Nhat Hanh

♪ *Notes from the Ocean*

Books and Authors I Treasure

Books are the carriers of civilization. Without books, history is silent. Literature dumb, science crippled, thought and speculation at standstill. Without books the development of a civilization would have been impossible. They are the engines of change, window on the world, lighthouses erected in the sea of time. They are the companions, teachers, magicians, bankers of the treasures of the mind. Books are humanity in print. —Barbara Tuchman

Some people think of reading only as a kind of escape. Books are much more. They are a way of being fully human. —Susan Sontag

The following writers/books captured my heart

Alan Lew: *One God Clapping, Be Still and Get Going, This Is Real and You Are Completely Unprepared*

Norman Fischer: *When You Greet Me I Bow, The World Could Be Otherwise*

Dr. Paula Bromberg: *The Way of the Lover, A Way of Understanding*

Yongey Mingyur Rinpoche: *In Love With The World*

Charlotte Joko Beck: *Ordinary Wonder, Everyday Zen*

P.D. Ouspensky: *Strange Life of Ivan Osokin*

Natalie Goldberg: *Writing Down The Bones, Three Simple Lines*

Books and Authors I Treasure

Daniel Ladinsky: *The Subject Tonight is Love, The Gift, Darling I Love You, The Purity of Desire, A Year With Hafiz, Love Poems from God*

Coleman Barks: *Naked Song Lalla*

Katherine Thanas: *The Truth of This Life*

Thich Nhat Hahn: *The Heart of Understanding, True Love*

Cooper Edens: *Caretakers of Wonder, If You're Afraid of the Dark Remember the Night Rainbow*

Dr. Gabor Mate: *The Myth of Normal*

Rami Shapiro: *Hasidic Tales*

Mary Oliver: *Dream Work, Devotions*

Florence Caplow, Susan Moon: *The Hidden Lamp*

Ranier Maria Rilke: *On Love and Other Difficulties*

Oscar Wilde: *The Happy Prince, The Selfish Giant*

Curt Leviant: *The Man Who Thought He Was Messiah*

Chris Griscom: *Ocean Born*

It seems to me that one should only read books which bite and sting one. If the book we are reading does not wake us up with a blow to the head, what's the point of reading? A book ought to be an ice pick to break up the frozen sea within us. —Franz Kafka

♪ *Notes from the Ocean*

Singing Creation Into Being
Opening Spirit to Celestial Music

Many say that life entered the human body by the help of music, but the truth is that life itself is music. —Hafiz

Music gives a Soul to the Universe Wings to the Mind Flight to the Imagination and Life to everything. —Plato

Music holds history, heritage and harmony of the soul making the world radiate. Breathing in melody, rhythm and sounds quiets the mind as well as builds stamina and life force. Music reveals the voice of soul. Music lives in the present moment. I sing and dance. The music continues throughout carrying me, holding spacious emptiness. The sound between the notes reverberate filling the atmosphere to return to the silence that is the true root of being.
—Dr. Paula Bromberg

The following musicians and music are wired to this heart-beat, my heart-song

Deva Premal and Miten

David Darling

Leonard Cohen

Gurdjieff chants and movements

Singing Creation Into Being

David Zeller

Natanel Goldberg

Luciano Pavarotti

Yiddish music

Broadway show tunes

To play a wrong note is insignificant, to play without passion is inexcusable. —Ludwig van Beethoven

Music was my refuge. I could crawl into the space between the notes and curl my back to loneliness. —Maya Angelou

There's a music for everything. Didn't you ever hear the earth spinning? It makes a sound like a humming top, Dear me, yes! Everything in the world—trees, rocks and stars and human beings—they all have their own true music. —P.L. Travers

May all that has been reduced to noise in you, become music again.

Thank You

A deep bow to the inspired teachers and wisdom-teachings quoted throughout this book. Use them well!

Gratitude to those whose lives I encounter, for their vulnerability and visibility, their opening and willingness.

Sashie my beloved soul-mate *It's a bonfire at midnight on the top edge of a hill, this meeting again with you.* Our lifetime together is a musical masterpiece of wonder. Gratitude to your artful dedication of love—a gift from the highest spheres. Your devotion and beautiful heart astound me! Who has created such gorgeousness—what a gift for the eye to behold! Alexandra, the reclining Buddha of immeasurable merits who captured my heart—the golden chalice—Apollonian form held steady for this Dionysian music.

Leslie Landy goddess of healing, Kwan Yin on a lotus petal, the body is our temple and your attentive lovingkindness and service inspires and extends the quality of my life. Thank you for your generous heart.

Elaine Marchese a lioness brave heart of kindness and integrity, capturing me when I stumbled, dignified and true to inner integrity.

Tom bringing musical wings through your flowing eye of order, I appreciate your sensibility, focus and

Thank You

dedication to the harmonious movement needed to create refinement: quality as perfection. And fun.

My life sister Iris Ruby, fraught with many wobbles, I have tempered and learned with great difficulty through these years to open in forgiveness embracing our differences.

Linda, smiling, singing, showing up with consistent kindness we journeyed through many waters together—wow, that would be another book! And here we are frayed at the edges, parts missing, with bigger more open heart.

Laya who walks in truth and modesty, my opera confidante, kindred spirit, you teach me that life in her expression touches and embraces the pulse of the other.

Scott compassionate and cherishing towards the children. You bring hope and light to this world. I treasure your beautiful heart and I love you.

Sanda and Bob—neighbors who evolved into loving family. The Mitzvot, deeds of kindness you both offer are an admirable flow of love.

Daya your fearless recognition of what is provides the space for what wants to happen. Embracing truth regardless offers me breathing room.

The beloveds who have penetrated my heart, releasing their earthly form: Mentor and friend artist with exalted vision Bonnie Whittingham, Mary Glassman,

♪ *Notes from the Ocean*

Adele and Manuel Bromberg, Dr. Harriet Rose Meiss, Dr. Elisabeth Kubler-Ross, Jean Robertson, Dr. Rona Lieberman, Joan Holode, Beth Weiner, Dr. Marsha Woolf, Heidi Kingsbury, Reshad Feild, Adnan Sarhan, Dr. Janine Canan, Robert Glazier. A deep bow to the mystery of the miraculous unknown. Yes, we are here walking each other home.

Deborah, grace and openness are the same.

Udbodha, our conversations are symphonies. This friendship a blessing and smile in my life.

To the great Mother Ocean who invites me to expand my vision, to deepen my practice and experience the open spaciousness of lifetimes.

Amma, garland of love, your smile enters this heart—your arms hold me.

To the lineage of universal laws that govern this universe, the invisible worlds that direct and protect us along a path of self-realization and Love.

May these teachings be received: they are intended for the benefit of all beings; service and love to repair our broken world, to lift heartache to a place of sweetness.

If the Beloved said pay homage to everything that has helped you enter my arms. There would not be one experience of my life, not one thought, not one feeling, not any act, I would not bow to. —Rumi

Further Continuing Work

Telephone sessions, E-mail and texts are available for self-study, inner investigation and personal growth. Mindful conversation, finding our voice our joy and sorrow brings deeper understanding enabling us to develop our practice of presence and live free from habituated conditioned patterns awakening to the sacred mystery of being. Contact through E-mail or Facebook:

Dr. Paula Bromberg

Goldoceandrive@gmail.com

Facebook: PaulaAmbikaBromberg

♪ *Notes from the Ocean*

About the Author

Dr. Paula Bromberg: Psychologist, Teacher, writer, lover of life, ocean-walker, inspired by her personal journey has experienced many paths, teachers, spiritual communities and methods. *Notes from the Ocean* draws on direct experience—both professional encounters and years of walking, singing in beautiful oceans and beaches throughout the world. Her books are written through an understanding that comes from decades of study, teaching, intimate conversation and digesting life experiences. Traveling and receiving initiation into Eastern and Western lineages: Sufi, Buddhist, Jewish, Gurdjieffian, East Indian; learning within living traditions, transcending formal boundaries to teach from those places and kindle a fire in the heart of others.

The author has a Doctorate in Philosophy in Clinical Psychology maintains a current telephone practice, recorded a live television series *Conversations with Dr Paula*. Her books, *The Way of the Lover*, *A Way of Understanding*, *The Fifth Way–Life at its Best* and *Notes from the Ocean, A Celebration of Love* are the foundation of her work. The living interconnectedness makes up the real world and all traditions are part of this way of being in the world. The creative force is love.

Paula was on the faculty of Northern New Mexico College co-creating and teaching the first University program with Dr. Elisabeth Kubler-Ross to educate and train hospice workers. She was interviewed and recorded by Dr. Zoe Lewis as a guest on her radio show *Health Through Knowledge*. As a consultant and frequent speaker for a regenerative medicine television series *My Medicine TV*, Dr. Bromberg also pioneered her own TV show *Conversations with Dr. Paula*.

She developed and created a psychological/spiritual system throughout her more than fifty years of working in conversation with people. To discover and study our essential nature; to experience the meaning and purpose of our life awakens us through concrete teachings that transform us to live our life mindfully, with presence. It is our birthright to be initiated into the truths that evoke the powers of our natural gifts enabling us to find hidden meaning and higher guidance inherent in our life.

From an early age Dr. Paula demonstrated an irrepressible striving to understand and to awaken. A voice of clarity and presence of heart Paula has written remarkable books of timeless wisdom that will change your life. Her work and writings have been praised by many of the foremost spiritual leaders from numerous traditions.

Dr. Paula says: *Personal identity appeared impossible— before I understood to be in the world and not of it. Form became a pliable construct, with the edges often bending and dropping away. Years passing by mirrors, no reflection, driven to move this body until collapsed into exhaustion;*

♪ *Notes from the Ocean*

passionate; initiated into invisibility, invisible threads, silver chord to the moon. Little sleep or rest. Years of practice to create a witness, someone home while dancing through this perilous wonder is the rope that tethered/tethers me from this heart to the heart of the universe. A devotee to Love, walking with the beloveds who dare risk and shatter form. This private experience, passionate, at times troublesome—living on the edge sometimes out of the margin, at times negligent to holding humanity in a container of love, I was protected throughout gathering experiences being in adventures and always the call to awaken as the greatest possibility—through a body that was driven to wake up.

Notes from the Ocean is destined to become another classic work, like *The Way of the Lover* the previous book—both bring clear insightful new understanding into the life of its reader. Beautifully written, you now hold in your hands a map to find treasure and the keys: practical wisdom for self-investigation.

Notes from the Ocean arrives after more than five decades of study, practice and listening. This great feast of love inspires and uplifts. It is dedicated to the teaching, understanding and freedom of all people. It is entertaining as well as depthful intended for those who love the creative process have used psychotherapy and other methods as a means of self-study and self-knowledge who recognize its limits and now want to awaken and satisfy the yearning for Truth, Love and

Beauty—that place beyond personality. No corner of the heart and mind to remain hidden or unexamined.

Notes from the Ocean is an invitation, encouragement and inspiration to open to our heart, to polish the mind, to investigate through self-inquiry uplifting our personal experiences to universal truths, the ordinary to become extraordinary.

With great integrity Dr. Bromberg takes you directly to your heart. A book of truth and power that will make a difference.

Lucky Life

Dear waves, what will you do for me this year? Will you drown out my scream? Will you let me rise through the fog? Will you fill me with that old salt feeling? Will you let me take my long steps in the cold sand? Will you let me lie on the white bedspread and study the black clouds with the blue holes in them? Will you let me see the rusty trees and the old monoplanes one more year? Will you let me draw my sacred figures and move the kites and birds around with my dark mind?

Lucky life is like this. Lucky there is an ocean to come to. Lucky you can judge yourself in this water. Lucky you can be purified over and over again. Lucky there is the same cleanliness for everyone. Lucky life is like that. Lucky life. Oh lucky life. Oh lucky lucky life. Lucky life. —Gerald Stern

♪ *Notes from the Ocean*

If you have time to chatter Read books
If you have time to read
Walk into mountain, desert and ocean
If you have time to walk
sing songs and dance
If you have time to dance
Sit quietly, you Happy Lucky Idiot.
—Nana Sakaki

    Learn through sitting at the feet of your own life
And did you get what you wanted from this life, even so?
I did.
And what did you want?
To call myself beloved,
To feel myself beloved on the earth.
—R. Carver

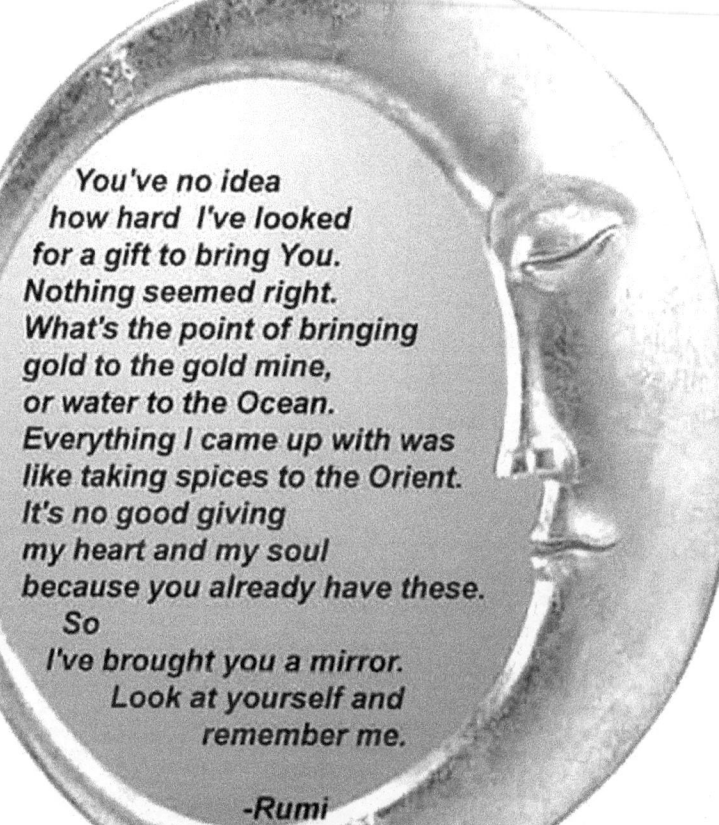

You've no idea
how hard I've looked
for a gift to bring You.
Nothing seemed right.
What's the point of bringing
gold to the gold mine,
or water to the Ocean.
Everything I came up with was
like taking spices to the Orient.
It's no good giving
my heart and my soul
because you already have these.
  So
I've brought you a mirror.
    Look at yourself and
        remember me.

            -Rumi